Elmwood Edition

THE COMPLETE WRITINGS OF
JAMES RUSSELL LOWELL

WITH PORTRAITS, ILLUSTRATIONS, AND FACSIMILES

IN SIXTEEN VOLUMES

VOLUME XIII

Mr. Lowell in 1889

THE POETICAL WORKS

OF

JAMES RUSSELL LOWELL

IN FIVE VOLUMES

VOLUME V

POEMS OF THE WAR
HEARTSEASE AND RUE
LAST POEMS

BOSTON AND NEW YORK
HOUGHTON, MIFFLIN AND COMPANY
The Riverside Press, Cambridge

CONTENTS

SENTIMENT

CONTENTS

viii CONTENTS

LIST OF ILLUSTRATIONS

POEMS OF THE WAR

THE WASHERS OF THE SHROUD

OCTOBER, 1861

ALONG a river-side, I know not where,
I walked one night in mystery of dream;
A chill creeps curdling yet beneath my hair,
To think what chanced me by the pallid gleam
Of a moon-wraith that waned through haunted air.

Pale fireflies pulsed within the meadow-mist
Their halos, wavering thistledowns of light;
The loon, that seemed to mock some goblin tryst,
Laughed; and the echoes, huddling in affright,
Like Odin's hounds, fled baying down the night.

Then all was silent, till there smote my ear
A movement in the stream that checked my breath:
Was it the slow plash of a wading deer?
But something said, " This water is of Death!
The Sisters wash a shroud, — ill thing to hear!"

I, looking then, beheld the ancient Three
Known to the Greek's and to the Northman's creed,
That sit in shadow of the mystic Tree,
Still crooning, as they weave their endless brede,
One song: " Time was, Time is, and Time shall be."

No wrinkled crones were they, as I had deemed,
But fair as yesterday, to-day, to-morrow,
To mourner, lover, poet, ever seemed;
Something too high for joy, too deep for sorrow,
Thrilled in their tones, and from their faces
    gleamed.

" Still men and nations reap as they have strawn,"
So sang they, working at their task the while;
" The fatal raiment must be cleansed ere dawn:
For Austria? 'Italy? the Sea-Queen's isle?
O'er what quenched grandeur must our shroud be
    drawn?

" Or is it for a younger, fairer corse,
That gathered States like children round his knees,
That tamed the wave to be his posting-horse,
Feller of forests, linker of the seas,
Bridge-builder, hammerer, youngest son of Thor's?

" What make we, murmur'st thou? and what are we?
When empires must be wound, we bring the shroud,
The time-old web of the implacable Three:
Is it too coarse for him, the young and proud?
Earth's mightiest deigned to wear it, — why not
    he?"

" Is there no hope?" I moaned, " so strong, so fair!
Our Fowler whose proud bird would brook erewhile
No rival's swoop in all our western air!
Gather the ravens, then, in funeral file
For him, life's morn yet golden in his hair?

" Leave me not hopeless, ye unpitying dames !
  I see, half seeing. Tell me, ye who scanned
  The stars, Earth's elders, still must noblest aims
  Be traced upon oblivious ocean-sands ?
  Must Hesper join the wailing ghosts of names ? "

" When grass-blades stiffen with red battle-dew,
  Ye deem we choose the victor and the slain :
  Say, choose we them that shall be leal and true
  To the heart's longing, the high faith of brain ?
  Yet there the victory lies, if ye but knew.

" Three roots bear up Dominion : Knowledge, Will, —
  These twain are strong, but stronger yet the third, —
  Obedience, — 't is the great tap-root that still,
  Knit round the rock of Duty, is not stirred,
  Though Heaven-loosed tempests spend their utmost skill.

" Is the doom sealed for Hesper ? 'T is not we
  Denounce it, but the Law before all time :
  The brave makes danger opportunity ;
  The waverer, paltering with the chance sublime,
  Dwarfs it to peril : which shall Hesper be ?

" Hath he let vultures climb his eagle's seat
  To make Jove's bolts purveyors of their maw ?
  Hath he the Many's plaudits found more sweet
  Than Wisdom ? held Opinion's wind for Law ?
  Then let him hearken for the doomster's feet !

" Rough are the steps, slow-hewn in flintiest rock,
   States climb to power by; slippery those with gold
Down which they stumble to eternal mock:
   No chafferer's hand shall long the sceptre hold,
Who, given a Fate to shape, would sell the block.

" We sing old Sagas, songs of weal and woe,
   Mystic because too cheaply understood;
Dark sayings are not ours; men hear and know,
   See Evil weak, see strength alone in Good,
Yet hope to stem God's fire with walls of tow.

" Time Was unlocks the riddle of Time Is,
   That offers choice of glory or of gloom;
The solver makes Time Shall Be surely his.
   But hasten, Sisters! for even now the tomb
Grates its slow hinge and calls from the abyss."

" But not for him," I cried, " not yet for him,
   Whose large horizon, westering, star by star
Wins from the void to where on Ocean's rim
   The sunset shuts the world with golden bar,
Not yet his thews shall fail, his eye grow dim!

" His shall be larger manhood, saved for those
   That walk unblenching through the trial-fires;
Not suffering, but faint heart, is worst of woes,
   And he no base-born son of craven sires,
Whose eye need blench confronted with his foes.

" Tears may be ours, but proud, for those who win
   Death's royal purple in the foeman's lines;

Peace, too, brings tears; and mid the battle-din,
The wiser ear some text of God divines,
For the sheathed blade may rust with darker sin.

" God, give us peace! not such as lulls to sleep,
But sword on thigh, and brow with purpose knit!
And let our Ship of State to harbor sweep,
Her ports all up, her battle-lanterns lit,
And her leashed thunders gathering for their leap!"

So cried I with clenched hands and passionate pain,
Thinking of dear ones by Potomac's side;
Again the loon laughed mocking, and again
The echoes bayed far down the night and died,
While waking I recalled my wandering brain

TWO SCENES FROM THE LIFE OF BLONDEL

AUTUMN, 1863

SCENE I. — *Near a castle in Germany*

'T WERE no hard task, perchance, to win
    The popular laurel for my song;
'T were only to comply with sin,
    And own the crown, though snatched by wrong:
Rather Truth's chaplet let me wear,
    Though sharp as death its thorns may sting;
Loyal to Loyalty, I bear
    No badge but of my rightful king.

Patient by town and tower I wait,
   Or o'er the blustering moorland go;
I buy no praise at cheaper rate,
   Or what faint hearts may fancy so;
For me, no joy in lady's bower,
   Or hall, or tourney, will I sing,
Till the slow stars wheel round the hour
   That crowns my hero and my king.

While all the land runs red with strife,
   And wealth is won by pedler-crimes,
Let who will find content in life
   And tinkle in unmanly rhymes;
I wait and seek; through dark and light,
   Safe in my heart my hope I bring,
Till I once more my faith may plight
   To him my whole soul owns her king.

When power is filched by drone and dolt,
   And, with caught breath and flashing eye,
Her knuckles whitening round the bolt,
   Vengeance leans eager from the sky,
While this and that the people guess,
   And to the skirts of praters cling,
Who court the crowd they should compress,
   I turn in scorn to seek my king.

Shut in what tower of darkling chance
   Or dungeon of a narrow doom,
Dream'st thou of battle-axe and lance
   That for the Cross make crashing room?

Come! with hushed breath the battle waits
    In the wild van thy mace's swing;
While doubters parley with their fates,
    Make thou thine own and ours, my king!

O, strong to keep upright the old,
    And wise to buttress with the new,
Prudent, as only are the bold,
    Clear-eyed, as only are the true,
To foes benign, to friendship stern,
    Intent to imp Law's broken wing,
Who would not die, if death might earn
    The right to kiss thy hand, my king?

SCENE II. — *An Inn near the Château of Chalus*

WELL, the whole thing is over, and here I sit
    With one arm in a sling and a milk-score of
        gashes,
And this flagon of Cyprus must e'en warm my wit,
    Since what's left of youth's flame is a head flecked
        with ashes.
I remember I sat in this very same inn, —
    I was young then, and one young man thought I
        was handsome, —
I had found out what prison King Richard was in,
    And was spurring for England to push on the
        ransom.

How I scorned the dull souls that sat guzzling
        around
    And knew not my secret nor recked my derision!

Let the world sink or swim, John or Richard be
   crowned,
   All one, so the beer-tax got lenient revision.
How little I dreamed, as I tramped up and down,
   That granting our wish one of Fate's saddest jokes
   is !
I had mine with a vengeance, — my king got his
   crown,
   And made his whole business to break other
   folks's.

I might as well join in the safe old *tum, tum :*
   A hero 's an excellent loadstar, — but, bless ye,
What infinite odds 'twixt a hero to come
   And your only too palpable hero *in esse !*
Precisely the odds (such examples are rife)
   'Twixt the poem conceived and the rhyme we
   make show of,
'Twixt the boy's morning dream and the wake-up of
   life,
   'Twixt the Blondel God meant and a Blondel I
   know of !

But the world 's better off, I 'm convinced of it
   now,
   Than if heroes, like buns, could be bought for a
   penny
To regard all mankind as their haltered milch-cow,
   And just care for themselves. Well, God cares for
   the many ;
For somehow the poor old Earth blunders along,
   Each son of hers adding his mite of unfitness,

And, choosing the sure way of coming out wrong,
  Gets to port as the next generation will witness.

You think her old ribs have come all crashing
    through,
  If a whisk of Fate's broom snap your cobweb asun-
    der ;
But her rivets were clinched by a wiser than you,
  And our sins cannot push the Lord's right hand
    from under.
Better one honest man who can wait for God's
    mind
  In our poor shifting scene here though heroes were
    plenty !
Better one bite, at forty, of Truth's bitter rind,
  Than the hot wine that gushed from the vintage of
    twenty !

I see it all now : when I wanted a king,
  'T was the kingship that failed in myself I was seek-
    · ing, —
'T is so much less easy to do than to sing,
  So much simpler to reign by a proxy than *be*
    king !
Yes, I think I *do* see : after all 's said and sung,
  Take this one rule of life and you never will rue
    it, —
'T is but do your own duty and hold your own
    tongue
  And Blondel were royal himself, if he knew it !

MEMORIÆ POSITUM

R. G. SHAW

I

BENEATH the trees,
  My lifelong friends in this dear spot,
  Sad now for eyes that see them not,
    I hear the autumnal breeze
Wake the dry leaves to sigh for gladness gone,
Whispering vague omens of oblivion,
    Hear, restless as the seas,
Time's grim feet rustling through the withered
      grace
Of many a spreading realm and strong-stemmed
      race,
    Even as my own through these.

    Why make we moan
  For loss that doth enrich us yet
  With upward yearnings of regret?
    Bleaker than unmossed stone
Our lives were but for this immortal gain
Of unstilled longing and inspiring pain!
    As thrills of long-hushed tone
Live in the viol, so our souls grow fine
With keen vibrations from the touch divine
    Of noble natures gone.

'T were indiscreet
To vex the shy and sacred grief
With harsh obtrusions of relief;
Yet, Verse, with noiseless feet,
Go whisper: "*This* death hath far choicer ends
Than slowly to impearl in hearts of friends;
These obsequies 't is meet
Not to seclude in closets of the heart,
But, church-like, with wide doorways, to impart
Even to the heedless street."

II

Brave, good, and true,
I see him stand before me now,
And read again on that young brow,
Where every hope was new,
How sweet were life! Yet, by the mouth firm-set,
And look made up for Duty's utmost debt,
I could divine he knew
That death within the sulphurous hostile lines,
In the mere wreck of nobly-pitched designs,
Plucks heartsease, and not rue.

Happy their end
Who vanish down life's evening stream
Placid as swans that drift in dream
Round the next river-bend!
Happy long life, with honor at the close,
Friends' painless tears, the softened thought of foes!
And yet, like him, to spend
All at a gush, keeping our first faith sure
From mid-life's doubt and eld's contentment poor,
What more could Fortune send?

Right in the van,
On the red rampart's slippery swell,
With heart that beat a charge, he fell
Foeward, as fits a man;
But the high soul burns on to light men's feet
Where death for noble ends makes dying sweet;
His life her crescent's span
Orbs full with share in their undarkening days
Who ever climbed the battailous steeps of praise
Since valor's praise began.

III

His life's expense
Hath won him coeternal youth
With the immaculate prime of Truth;
While we, who make pretence
At living on, and wake and eat and sleep,
And life's stale trick by repetition keep,
Our fickle permanence
(A poor leaf-shadow on a brook, whose play
Of busy idlesse ceases with our day)
Is the mere cheat of sense.

We bide our chance,
Unhappy, and make terms with Fate
A little more to let us wait;
He leads for aye the advance,
Hope's forlorn-hopes that plant the desperate good
For nobler Earths and days of manlier mood;
Our wall of circumstance
Cleared at a bound, he flashes o'er the fight,
A saintly shape of fame, to cheer the right
And steel each wavering glance.

I write of one,
While with dim eyes I think of three;
Who weeps not others fair and brave as he?
Ah, when the fight is won,
Dear Land, whom triflers now make bold to scorn
(Thee! from whose forehead Earth awaits her morn),
How nobler shall the sun
Flame in thy sky, how braver breathe thy air,
That thou bred'st children who for thee could dare
And die as thine have done!

1863.

ON BOARD THE '76

WRITTEN FOR MR. BRYANT'S SEVENTIETH BIRTHDAY

NOVEMBER 3, 1864

OUR ship lay tumbling in an angry sea,
Her rudder gone, her mainmast o'er the side;
Her scuppers, from the waves' clutch staggering free,
Trailed threads of priceless crimson through the tide;
Sails, shrouds, and spars with pirate cannon torn,
We lay, awaiting morn.

Awaiting morn, such morn as mocks despair;
And she that bare the promise of the world
Within her sides, now hopeless, helmless, bare,
At random o'er the wildering waters hurled;
The reek of battle drifting slow alee
Not sullener than we.

Morn came at last to peer into our woe,
   When lo, a sail! Now surely help was nigh;
The red cross flames aloft, Christ's pledge; but
     no,
   Her black guns grinning hate, she rushes by
And hails us:— "Gains the leak! Ay, so we
     thought!
     Sink, then, with curses fraught!"

I leaned against my gun still angry-hot,
   And my lids tingled with the tears held back;
This scorn methought was crueller than shot:
   The manly death-grip in the battle-wrack,
Yard-arm to yard-arm, were more friendly far
     Than such fear-smothered war.

There our foe wallowed, like a wounded brute
   The fiercer for his hurt. What now were best?
Once more tug bravely at the peril's root,
   Though death came with it? Or evade the test
If right or wrong in this God's world of ours
     Be leagued with mightier powers?

Some, faintly loyal, felt their pulses lag
   With the slow beat that doubts and then de-
     spairs;
Some, caitiff, would have struck the starry flag
   That knits us with our past, and makes us
     heirs
Of deeds high-hearted as were ever done
     'Neath the all-seeing sun.

But there was one, the Singer of our crew,
  Upon whose head Age waved his peaceful
    sign,
But whose red heart's-blood no surrender knew;
  And couchant under brows of massive line,
The eyes, like guns beneath a parapet,
    Watched, charged with lightnings yet.

The voices of the hills did his obey;
  The torrents flashed and tumbled in his song;
He brought our native fields from far away,
  Or set us 'mid the innumerable throng
Of dateless woods, or where we heard the calm
    Old homestead's evening psalm.

But now he sang of faith to things unseen,
  Of freedom's birthright given to us in trust;
And words of doughty cheer he spoke between,
  That made all earthly fortune seem as dust,
Matched with that duty, old as Time and new,
    Of being brave and true.

We, listening, learned what makes the might of
    words, —
  Manhood to back them, constant as a star;
His voice rammed home our cannon, edged our
    swords,
    And sent our boarders shouting; shroud and
      spar
Heard him and stiffened; the sails heard, and wooed
    The winds with loftier mood.

  v

In our dark hours he manned our guns again;
 Remanned ourselves from his own manhood's
  stores;
Pride, honor, country, throbbed through all his strain;
 And shall we praise? God's praise was his before;
And on our futile laurels he looks down,
  Himself our bravest crown.

ODE RECITED AT THE HARVARD COMMEMORATION

JULY 21, 1865

I

WEAK-WINGED is song,
Nor aims at that clear-ethered height
Whither the brave deed climbs for light:
 We seem to do them wrong,
Bringing our robin's-leaf to deck their hearse
Who in warm life-blood wrote their nobler verse,
Our trivial song to honor those who come
With ears attuned to strenuous trump and drum,
And shaped in squadron-strophes their desire,
Live battle-odes whose lines were steel and fire:
 Yet sometimes feathered words are strong,
A gracious memory to buoy up and save
From Lethe's dreamless ooze, the common grave
  Of the unventurous throng.

II

To-day our Reverend Mother welcomes back
  Her wisest Scholars, those who understood
The deeper teaching of her mystic tome,
    And offered their fresh lives to make it good :
        No lore of Greece or Rome,
No science peddling with the names of things,
Or reading stars to find inglorious fates,
        Can lift our life with wings
Far from Death's idle gulf that for the many waits,
        And lengthen out our dates
With that clear fame whose memory sings
In manly hearts to come, and nerves them and dilates :
Nor such thy teaching, Mother of us all !
        Not such the trumpet-call
        Of thy diviner mood,
        That could thy sons entice
From happy homes and toils, the fruitful nest
Of those half-virtues which the world calls best,
        Into War's tumult rude ;
        But rather far that stern device
The sponsors chose that round thy cradle stood
        In the dim, unventured wood,
        The VERITAS that lurks beneath
        The letter's unprolific sheath,
  Life of whate'er makes life worth living,
Seed-grain of high emprise, immortal food,
  One heavenly thing whereof earth hath the giving.

III

Many loved Truth, and lavished life's best oil
  Amid the dust of books to find her,

Content at last, for guerdon of their toil,
  With the cast mantle she hath left behind her.
    Many in sad faith sought for her,
    Many with crossed hands sighed for her;
    But these, our brothers, fought for her;
    At life's dear peril wrought for her,
    So loved her that they died for her,
    Tasting the raptured fleetness
    Of her divine completeness:
      Their higher instinct knew
Those love her best who to themselves are true,
And what they dare to dream of, dare to do;
    They followed her and found her
    Where all may hope to find,
Not in the ashes of the burnt-out mind,
But beautiful, with danger's sweetness round her.
    Where faith made whole with deed
    Breathes its awakening breath
    Into the lifeless creed,
    They saw her plumed and mailed,
    With sweet, stern face unveiled,
And all-repaying eyes, look proud on them in death.

IV

Our slender life runs rippling by, and glides
  Into the silent hollow of the past;
    What is there that abides
  To make the next age better for the last?
    Is earth too poor to give us
  Something to live for here that shall outlive us?
    Some more substantial boon

Than such as flows and ebbs with Fortune's fickle
      moon?
    The little that we see
    From doubt is never free;
    The little that we do
    Is but half-nobly true;
    With our laborious hiving
What men call treasure, and the gods call dross,
  Life seems a jest of Fate's contriving,
  Only secure in every one's conniving,
A long account of nothings paid with loss,
Where we poor puppets, jerked by unseen wires,
  After our little hour of strut and rave,
With all our pasteboard passions and desires,
Loves, hates, ambitions, and immortal fires,
  Are tossed pell-mell together in the grave.
  But stay! no age was e'er degenerate,
  Unless men held it at too cheap a rate,
  For in our likeness still we shape our fate.
    Ah, there is something here
  Unfathomed by the cynic's sneer,
  Something that gives our feeble light
  A high immunity from Night,
  Something that leaps life's narrow bars
To claim its birthright with the hosts of heaven;
  A seed of sunshine that can leaven
  Our earthly dulness with the beams of stars,
    And glorify our clay
With light from fountains elder than the Day;
    A conscience more divine than we,
    A gladness fed with secret tears,
    A vexing, forward-reaching sense

Of some more noble permanence;
A light across the sea,
Which haunts the soul and will not let it be,
Still beaconing from the heights of undegenerate years.

v

Whither leads the path
To ampler fates that leads?
Not down through flowery meads,
To reap an aftermath
Of youth's vainglorious weeds,
But up the steep, amid the wrath
And shock of deadly-hostile creeds,
Where the world's best hope and stay
By battle's flashes gropes a desperate way,
And every turf the fierce foot clings to bleeds.
Peace hath her not ignoble wreath,
Ere yet the sharp, decisive word
Light the black lips of cannon, and the sword
Dreams in its easeful sheath;
But some day the live coal behind the thought,
Whether from Baäl's stone obscene,
Or from the shrine serene
Of God's pure altar brought,
Bursts up in flame; the war of tongue and pen
Learns with what deadly purpose it was fraught,
And, helpless in the fiery passion caught,
Shakes all the pillared state with shock of men;
Some day the soft Ideal that we wooed
Confronts us fiercely, foe-beset, pursued,
And cries reproachful: "Was it, then, my praise,

And not myself was loved ? Prove now thy truth ;
I claim of thee the promise of thy youth ;
Give me thy life, or cower in empty phrase,
The victim of thy genius, not its mate ! "
   Life may be given in many ways,
   And loyalty to Truth be sealed
As bravely in the closet as the field,
     So bountiful is Fate ;
     But then to stand beside her,
     When craven churls deride her,
To front a lie in arms and not to yield,
     This shows, methinks, God's plan
     And measure of a stalwart man,
     Limbed like the old heroic breeds,
     Who stands self-poised on manhood's solid earth,
     Not forced to frame excuses for his birth,
Fed from within with all the strength he needs.

VI

Such was he, our Martyr-Chief,
     Whom late the Nation he had led,
     With ashes on her head,   •
Wept with the passion of an angry grief :
Forgive me, if from present things I turn
To speak what in my heart will beat and burn,
And hang my wreath on his world-honored urn.
     Nature, they say, doth dote,
     And cannot make a man
     Save on some worn-out plan,
     Repeating us by rote :
For him her Old-World moulds aside she threw,

And, choosing sweet clay from the breast
      Of the unexhausted West,
With stuff untainted shaped a hero new,
Wise, steadfast in the strength of God, and true.
      How beautiful to see
Once more a shepherd of mankind indeed,
Who loved his charge, but never loved to lead;
One whose meek flock the people joyed to be,
      Not lured by any cheat of birth,
      But by his clear-grained human worth,
And brave old wisdom of sincerity!
      They knew that outward grace is dust;
      They could not choose but trust
In that sure-footed mind's unfaltering skill,
      And supple-tempered will
That bent like perfect steel to spring again and
      thrust.
      His was no lonely mountain-peak of mind,
      Thrusting to thin air o'er our cloudy bars,
      A sea-mark now, now lost in vapors blind;
      Broad prairie rather, genial, level-lined,
      Fruitful and friendly for all human kind,
Yet also nigh to heaven and loved of loftiest stars.
      Nothing of Europe here,
Or, then, of Europe fronting mornward still,
      Ere any names of Serf and Peer
      Could Nature's equal scheme deface
      And thwart her genial will;
      Here was a type of the true elder race,
And one of Plutarch's men talked with us face to
      face.
      I praise him not; it were too late;

And some innative weakness there must be
In him who condescends to victory
Such as the Present gives, and cannot wait,
  Safe in himself as in a fate.
   So always firmly he:
   He knew to bide his time,
   And can his fame abide,
Still patient in his simple faith sublime,
   Till the wise years decide.
 Great captains, with their guns and drums,
  Disturb our judgment for the hour,
   But at last silence comes;
 These all are gone, and, standing like a tower,
Our children shall behold his fame,
 The kindly-earnest, brave, foreseeing man,
Sagacious, patient, dreading praise, not blame,
 New birth of our new soil, the first American.

VII

 Long as man's hope insatiate can discern
  Or only guess some more inspiring goal
  Outside of Self, enduring as the pole,
Along whose course the flying axles burn
Of spirits bravely-pitched, earth's manlier brood;
  Long as below we cannot find
 The meed that stills the inexorable mind;
 So long this faith to some ideal Good,
 Under whatever mortal names it masks,
 Freedom, Law, Country, this ethereal mood
That thanks the Fates for their severer tasks,
 Feeling its challenged pulses leap,

While others skulk in subterfuges cheap,
And, set in Danger's van, has all the boon it asks,
  Shall win man's praise and woman's love,
  Shall be a wisdom that we set above
All other skills and gifts to culture dear,
  A virtue round whose forehead we inwreathe
  Laurels that with a living passion breathe
When other crowns grow, while we twine them, sear.
  What brings us thronging these high rites to pay,
And seal these hours the noblest of our year,
  Save that our brothers found this better way?

VIII

We sit here in the Promised Land
  That flows with Freedom's honey and milk:
  But 't was they won it, sword in hand,
Making the nettle danger soft for us as silk.
  We welcome back our bravest and our best; —
  Ah me! not all! some come not with the rest,
Who went forth brave and bright as any here!
I strive to mix some gladness with my strain,
        But the sad strings complain,
        And will not please the ear:
I sweep them for a pæan, but they wane
        Again and yet again
Into a dirge, and die away, in pain.
In these brave ranks I only see the gaps,
Thinking of dear ones whom the dumb turf wraps,
Dark to the triumph which they died to gain:
    Fitlier may others greet the living,
    For me the past is unforgiving;

I with uncovered head
Salute the sacred dead,
Who went, and who return not. — Say not so!
'T is not the grapes of Canaan that repay,
But the high faith that failed not by the way;
Virtue treads paths that end not in the grave;
No ban of endless night exiles the brave;
And to the saner mind
We rather seem the dead that stayed behind.
Blow, trumpets, all your exultations blow!
For never shall their aureoled presence lack:
I see them muster in a gleaming row,
With ever-youthful brows that nobler show;
We find in our dull road their shining track;
In every nobler mood
We feel the orient of their spirit glow,
Part of our life's unalterable good,
Of all our saintlier aspiration;
They come transfigured back,
Secure from change in their high-hearted ways,
Beautiful evermore, and with the rays
Of morn on their white Shields of Expectation!

IX

But is there hope to save
Even this ethereal essence from the grave?
What ever 'scaped Oblivion's subtle wrong
Save a few clarion names, or golden threads of
song?
Before my musing eye
The mighty ones of old sweep by,

Disvoicĕd now and insubstantial things,
As noisy once as we; poor ghosts of kings,
Shadows of empire wholly gone to dust,
And many races, nameless long ago,
To darkness driven by that imperious gust
Of ever-rushing Time that here doth blow:
O visionary world, condition strange,
Where naught abiding is but only Change,
Where the deep-bolted stars themselves still shift and
      range!
Shall we to more continuance make pretence?
Renown builds tombs; a life-estate is Wit;
      And, bit by bit,
The cunning years steal all from us but woe;
   Leaves are we, whose decays no harvest sow.
      But, when we vanish hence,
   Shall they lie forceless in the dark below,
   Save to make green their little length of sods,
   Or deepen pansies for a year or two,
   Who now to us are shining-sweet as gods?
   Was dying all they had the skill to do?
   That were not fruitless: but the Soul resents
   Such short-lived service, as if blind events
   Ruled without her, or earth could so endure;
   She claims a more divine investiture
   Of longer tenure than Fame's airy rents;
   Whate'er she touches doth her nature share;
   Her inspiration haunts the ennobled air,
      Gives eyes to mountains blind,
   Ears to the deaf earth, voices to the wind,
   And her clear trump sings succor everywhere
   By lonely bivouacs to the wakeful mind;
   For soul inherits all that soul could dare:

Memorial Hall

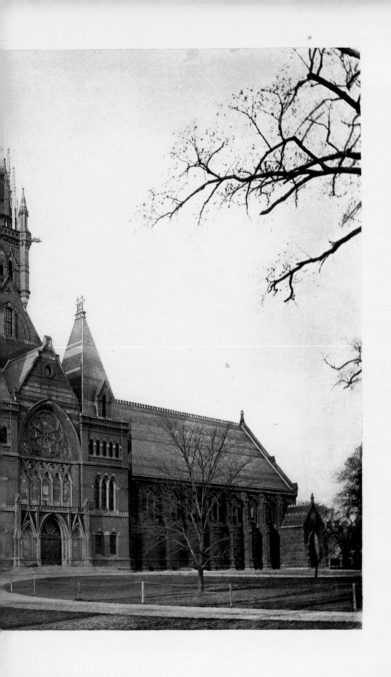

Yea, Manhood hath a wider span
And larger privilege of life than man.
The single deed, the private sacrifice,
So radiant now through proudly-hidden tears,
Is covered up ere long from mortal eyes
With thoughtless drift of the deciduous years;
But that high privilege that makes all men peers,
That leap of heart whereby a people rise
Up to a noble anger's height,
And, flamed on by the Fates, not shrink, but grow
more bright,
That swift validity in noble veins,
Of choosing danger and disdaining shame,
Of being set on flame
By the pure fire that flies all contact base,
But wraps its chosen with angelic might,
These are imperishable gains,
Sure as the sun, medicinal as light,
These hold great futures in their lusty reins
And certify to earth a new imperial race.

x

Who now shall sneer?
Who dare again to say we trace
Our lines to a plebeian race?
Roundhead and Cavalier!
Dumb are those names erewhile in battle loud;
Dream-footed as the shadow of a cloud,
They flit across the ear:
That is best blood that hath most iron in 't,
To edge resolve with, pouring without stint
For what makes manhood dear.

Tell us not of Plantagenets,
Hapsburgs, and Guelfs, whose thin bloods crawl
Down from some victor in a border-brawl!

How poor their outworn coronets,
Matched with one leaf of that plain civic wreath
Our brave for honor's blazon shall bequeath,

Through whose desert a rescued Nation sets
Her heel on treason, and the trumpet hears
Shout victory, tingling Europe's sullen ears

With vain resentments and more vain regrets!

XI

Not in anger, not in pride,
Pure from passion's mixture rude
Ever to base earth allied,
But with far-heard gratitude,
Still with heart and voice renewed,
To heroes living and dear martyrs dead,
The strain should close that consecrates our brave.
Lift the heart and lift the head!
Lofty be its mood and grave,
Not without a martial ring,
Not without a prouder tread
And a peal of exultation :
Little right has he to sing
Through whose heart in such an hour
Beats no march of conscious power,
Sweeps no tumult of elation!
'T is no Man we celebrate,
By his country's victories great,
A hero half, and half the whim of Fate,

But the pith and marrow of a Nation
Drawing force from all her men,
Highest, humblest, weakest, all,
For her time of need, and then
Pulsing it again through them,
Till the basest can no longer cower,
Feeling his soul spring up divinely tall,
Touched but in passing by her mantle-hem.
Come back, then, noble pride, for 't is her dower!
        How could poet ever tower,
        If his passions, hopes, and fears,
        If his triumphs and his tears,
        Kept not measure with his people?
Boom, cannon, boom to all the winds and waves!
Clash out, glad bells, from every rocking steeple!
Banners, a-dance with triumph, bend your staves!
    And from every mountain-peak
    Let beacon-fire to answering beacon speak,
    Katahdin tell Monadnock, Whiteface he,
And so leap on in light from sea to sea,
        Till the glad news be sent
        Across a kindling continent,
Making earth feel more firm and air breathe braver:
" Be proud! for she is saved, and all have helped to
            save her!
    She that lifts up the manhood of the poor,
    She of the open soul and open door,
    With room about her hearth for all mankind!
    The fire is dreadful in her eyes no more;
    From her bold front the helm she doth unbind,
    Sends all her handmaid armies back to spin,
    And bids her navies, that so lately hurled

Their crashing battle, hold their thunders in,
Swimming like birds of calm along the unharm-
    ful shore.
No challenge sends she to the elder world,
  That looked askance and hated; a light scorn
  Plays o'er her mouth, as round her mighty knees
  She calls her children back, and waits the morn
Of nobler day, enthroned between her subject seas."

XII

Bow down, dear Land, for thou hast found release!
  Thy God, in these distempered days,
  Hath taught thee the sure wisdom of His ways,
And through thine enemies hath wrought thy peace!
    Bow down in prayer and praise!
No poorest in thy borders but may now
Lift to the juster skies a man's enfranchised brow.
O Beautiful! my Country! ours once more!
Smoothing thy gold of war-dishevelled hair
O'er such sweet brows as never other wore,
    And letting thy set lips,
    Freed from wrath's pale eclipse,
The rosy edges of their smile lay bare,
What words divine of lover or of poet
Could tell our love and make thee know it,
Among the Nations bright beyond compare?
    What were our lives without thee?
    What all our lives to save thee?
    We reck not what we gave thee;
    We will not dare to doubt thee,
But ask whatever else, and we will dare!

L'ENVOI

TO THE MUSE

WHITHER ? Albeit I follow fast,
  In all life's circuit I but find,
Not where thou art, but where thou wast,
  Sweet beckoner, more fleet than wind !
I haunt the pine-dark solitudes,
  With soft brown silence carpeted,
And plot to snare thee in the woods :
  Peace I o'ertake, but thou art fled !
I find the rock where thou didst rest,
The moss thy skimming foot hath prest ;
  All Nature with thy parting thrills,
Like branches after birds new-flown ;
  Thy passage hill and hollow fills
With hints of virtue not their own ;
In dimples still the water slips
Where thou hast dipt thy finger-tips ;
  Just, just beyond, forever burn
  Gleams of a grace without return ;
  Upon thy shade I plant my foot,
And through my frame strange raptures shoot ;
All of thee but thyself I grasp ;
  I seem to fold thy luring shape,
And vague air to my bosom clasp,
  Thou lithe, perpetual Escape !
One mask and then another drops,
And thou art secret as before :

Sometimes with flooded ear I list,
And hear thee, wondrous organist,
From mighty continental stops
A thunder of new music pour;
Through pipes of earth and air and stone
Thy inspiration deep is blown;
Through mountains, forests, open downs,
Lakes, railroads, prairies, states, and towns,
Thy gathering fugue goes rolling on
From Maine to utmost Oregon;
The factory-wheels in cadence hum,
From brawling parties concords come;
All this I hear, or seem to hear,
But when, enchanted, I draw near
To mate with words the various theme,
Life seems a whiff of kitchen steam,
History an organ-grinder's thrum,
    For thou hast slipt from it and me
And all thine organ-pipes left dumb,
    Most mutable Perversity!

Not weary yet, I still must seek,
And hope for luck next day, next week;
I go to see the great man ride,
Shiplike, the swelling human tide
That floods to bear him into port,
Trophied from Senate-hall and Court;
Thy magnetism, I feel it there,
Thy rhythmic presence fleet and rare,
Making the Mob a moment fine
With glimpses of their own Divine,
As in their demigod they see

Their cramped ideal soaring free;
'T was thou didst bear the fire about,
  That, like the springing of a mine
Sent up to heaven the street-long shout;
Full well I know that thou wast here,
It was thy breath that brushed my ear;
But vainly in the stress and whirl
I dive for thee, the moment's pearl.

Through every shape thou well canst run,
Proteus, 'twixt rise and set of sun,
Well pleased with logger-camps in Maine
  As where Milan's pale Duomo lies
A stranded glacier on the plain,
  Its peaks and pinnacles of ice
  Melted in many a quaint device
And sees, above the city's din,
Afar its silent Alpine kin:
I track thee over carpets deep
To wealth's and beauty's inmost keep;
Across the sand of bar-room floors,
Mid the stale reek of boosing boors;
Where drowse the hay-field's fragrant heats,
Or the flail-heart of Autumn beats;
I dog thee through the market's throngs
To where the sea with myriad tongues
Laps the green edges of the pier,
And the tall ships that eastward steer,
Curtsy their farewells to the town,
O'er the curved distance lessening down;
I follow allwhere for thy sake;
Touch thy robe's hem, but ne'er o'ertake,

Find where, scarce yet unmoving, lies,
Warm from thy limbs, thy last disguise;
But thou another shape hast donned,
And lurest still just, just beyond!

But here a voice, I know not whence,
Thrills clearly through my inward sense,
Saying: "See where she sits at home
While thou in search of her dost roam!
All summer long her ancient wheel
    Whirls humming by the open door,
Or, when the hickory's social zeal
    Sets the wide chimney in a roar,
Close-nestled by the tinkling hearth,
It modulates the household mirth
With that sweet serious undertone
Of duty, music all her own;
Still as of old she sits and spins
Our hopes, our sorrows, and our sins;
With equal care she twines the fates
Of cottages and mighty states;
She spins the earth, the air, the sea,
The maiden's unschooled fancy free,
The boy's first love, the man's first grief,
The budding and the fall o' the leaf;
The piping west-wind's snowy care
For her their cloudy fleeces spare,
Or from the thorns of evil times
She can glean wool to twist her rhymes;
Morning and noon and eve supply
To her their fairest tints for dye,

But ever through her twirling thread
There spires one line of warmest red,
Tinged from the homestead's genial heart,
The stamp and warrant of her art;
With this Time's sickle she outwears,
And blunts the Sisters' baffled shears.

'' Harass her not : thy heat and stir
But greater coyness breed in her;
Yet thou mayst find, ere Age's frost,
Thy long apprenticeship not lost,
Learning at last that Stygian Fate
Unbends to him that knows to wait.
The Muse is womanish, nor deigns
Her love to him that pules and plains;
With proud, averted face she stands
To him that wooes with empty hands.
Make thyself free of Manhood's guild;
Pull down thy barns and greater build;
The wood, the mountain, and the plain
Wave breast-deep with the poet's grain;
Pluck thou the sunset's fruit of gold,
Glean from the heavens and ocean old;
From fireside lone and trampling street
Let thy life garner daily wheat;
The epic of a man rehearse,
Be something better than thy verse;
Make thyself rich, and then the Muse
Shall court thy precious interviews,
Shall take thy head upon her knee,
And such enchantment lilt to thee,

That thou shalt hear the life-blood flow
From farthest stars to grass-blades low,
And find the Listener's science still
Transcends the Singer's deepest skill!"

THE CATHEDRAL

To

MR. JAMES T. FIELDS

My Dear Fields :

Dr. Johnson's sturdy self-respect led him to invent the Bookseller as a substitute for the Patron. My relations with you have enabled me to discover how pleasantly the Friend may replace the Bookseller. Let me record my sense of many thoughtful services by associating your name with a poem which owes its appearance in this form to your partiality.

Cordially yours,

J. R. LOWELL.

Cambridge, *November* 29, 1869.

THE CATHEDRAL

FAR through the memory shines a happy day,
Cloudless of care, down-shod to every sense,
And simply perfect from its own resource,
As to a bee the new campanula's
Illuminate seclusion swung in air.
Such days are not the prey of setting suns,
Nor ever blurred with mist of afterthought;
Like words made magical by poets dead,
Wherein the music of all meaning is
The sense hath garnered or the soul divined,
They mingle with our life's ethereal part,
Sweetening and gathering sweetness evermore,
By beauty's franchise disenthralled of time.

I can recall, nay, they are present still,
Parts of myself, the perfume of my mind,
Days that seem farther off than Homer's now
Ere yet the child had loudened to the boy,
And I, recluse from playmates, found perforce
Companionship in things that not denied
Nor granted wholly; as is Nature's wont,
Who, safe in uncontaminate reserve,
Lets us mistake our longing for her love,
And mocks with various echo of ourselves.

These first sweet frauds upon our consciousness,
That blend the sensual with its imaged world,

These virginal cognitions, gifts of morn,
Ere life grow noisy, and slower-footed thought
Can overtake the rapture of the sense,
To thrust between ourselves and what we feel,
Have something in them secretly divine.
Vainly the eye, once schooled to serve the brain,
With pains deliberate studies to renew
The ideal vision : second thoughts are prose;
For beauty's acme hath a term as brief
As the wave's poise before it break in pearl.
Our own breath dims the mirror of the sense,
Looking too long and closely : at a flash
We snatch the essential grace of meaning out,
And that first passion beggars all behind,
Heirs of a tamer transport prepossessed.
Who, seeing once, has truly seen again
The gray vague of unsympathizing sea
That dragged his Fancy from her moorings back
To shores inhospitable of eldest time,
Till blank foreboding of earth-gendered powers,
Pitiless seignories in the elements,
Omnipotences blind that darkling smite,
Misgave him, and repaganized the world ?
Yet, by some subtler touch of sympathy,
These primal apprehensions, dimly stirred,
Perplex the eye with pictures from within.
This hath made poets dream of lives foregone
In worlds fantastical, more fair than ours ;
So Memory cheats us, glimpsing half-revealed.
Even as I write she tries her wonted spell
In that continuous redbreast boding rain :
The bird I hear sings not from yonder elm ;

But the flown ecstasy my childhood heard
Is vocal in my mind, renewed by him,
Haply made sweeter by the accumulate thrill
That threads my undivided life and steals
A pathos from the years and graves between.

I know not how it is with other men,
Whom I but guess, deciphering myself;
For me, once felt is so felt nevermore.
The fleeting relish at sensation's brim
Had in it the best ferment of the wine.
One spring I knew as never any since:
All night the surges of the warm southwest
Boomed intermittent through the wallowing elms,
And brought a morning from the Gulf adrift,
Omnipotent with sunshine, whose quick charm
Startled with crocuses the sullen turf
And wiled the bluebird to his whiff of song:
One summer hour abides, what time I perched,
Dappled with noonday, under simmering leaves,
And pulled the pulpy oxhearts, while aloof
An oriole clattered and the robins shrilled,
Denouncing me an alien and a thief:
One morn of autumn lords it o'er the rest,
When in the lane I watched the ash-leaves fall,
Balancing softly earthward without wind,
Or twirling with directer impulse down
On those fallen yesterday, now barbed with frost,
While I grew pensive with the pensive year:
And once I learned how marvellous winter was,
When past the fence-rails, downy-gray with rime,
I creaked adventurous o'er the spangled crust

That made familiar fields seem far and strange
As those stark wastes that whiten endlessly
In ghastly solitude about the pole,
And gleam relentless to the unsetting sun:
Instant the candid chambers of my brain
Were painted with these sovran images;
And later visions seem but copies pale
From those unfading frescos of the past,
Which I, young savage, in my age of flint,
Gazed at, and dimly felt a power in me
Parted from Nature by the joy in her
That doubtfully revealed me to myself.
Thenceforward I must stand outside the gate;
And paradise was paradise the more,
Known once and barred against satiety.

What we call Nature, all outside ourselves,
Is but our own conceit of what we see,
Our own reaction upon what we feel;
The world 's a woman to our shifting mood,
Feeling with us, or making due pretence;
And therefore we the more persuade ourselves
To make all things our thought's confederates,
Conniving with us in whate'er we dream.
So when our Fancy seeks analogies,
Though she have hidden what she after finds,
She loves to cheat herself with feigned surprise.
I find my own complexion everywhere:
No rose, I doubt, was ever, like the first,
A marvel to the bush it dawned upon,
The rapture of its life made visible,
The mystery of its yearning realized,

As the first babe to the first woman born;
No falcon ever felt delight of wings
As when, an eyas, from the stolid cliff
Loosing himself, he followed his high heart
To swim on sunshine, masterless as wind;
And I believe the brown earth takes delight
In the new snowdrop looking back at her,
To think that by some vernal alchemy
It could transmute her darkness into pearl;
What is the buxom peony after that,
With its coarse constancy of hoyden blush?
What the full summer to that wonder new?

But, if in nothing else, in us there is
A sense fastidious hardly reconciled
To the poor makeshifts of life's scenery,
Where the same slide must double all its parts,
Shoved in for Tarsus and hitched back for Tyre.
I blame not in the soul this daintiness,
Rasher of surfeit than a humming-bird,
In things indifferent by sense purveyed;
It argues her an immortality
And dateless incomes of experience,
This unthrift housekeeping that will not brook
A dish warmed-over at the feast of life,
And finds Twice stale, served with whatever sauce.
Nor matters much how it may go with me
Who dwell in Grub Street and am proud to drudge
Where men, my betters, wet their crust with tears:
Use can make sweet the peach's shady side,
That only by reflection tastes of sun.

But she, my Princess, who will sometimes deign
My garret to illumine till the walls,
Narrow and dingy, scrawled with hackneyed thought
(Poor Richard slowly elbowing Plato out),
Dilate and drape themselves with tapestries
Nausikaa might have stooped o'er, while, between,
Mirrors, effaced in their own clearness, send
Her only image on through deepening deeps
With endless repercussion of delight, —
Bringer of life, witching each sense to soul,
That sometimes almost gives me to believe
I might have been a poet, gives at least
A brain desaxonized, an ear that makes
Music where none is, and a keener pang
Of exquisite surmise outleaping thought, —
Her will I pamper in her luxury :
No crumpled rose-leaf of too careless choice
Shall bring a northern nightmare to her dreams,
Vexing with sense of exile ; hers shall be
The invitiate firstlings of experience,
Vibrations felt but once and felt life long.
Oh, more than halfway turn that Grecian front
Upon me, while with self-rebuke I spell,
On the plain fillet that confines thy hair
In conscious bounds of seeming unconstraint,
The *Naught in overplus*, thy race's badge !

One feast for her I secretly designed
In that Old World so strangely beautiful
To us the disinherited of eld, —
A day at Chartres, with no soul beside
To roil with pedant prate my joy serene

And make the minster shy of confidence.
I went, and, with the Saxon's pious care,
First ordered dinner at the pea-green inn,
The flies and I its only customers.
Eluding these, I loitered through the town,
With hope to take my minster unawares
In its grave solitude of memory.
A pretty burgh, and such as Fancy loves
For bygone grandeurs, faintly rumorous now
Upon the mind's horizon, as of storm
Brooding its dreamy thunders far aloof,
That mingle with our mood, but not disturb.
Its once grim bulwarks, tamed to lovers' walks,
Look down unwatchful on the sliding Eure,
Whose listless leisure suits the quiet place,
Lisping among his shallows homelike sounds
At Concord and by Bankside heard before.
Chance led me to a public pleasure-ground,
Where I grew kindly with the merry groups,
And blessed the Frenchman for his simple art
Of being domestic in the light of day.
His language has no word, we growl, for Home;
But he can find a fireside in the sun,
Play with his child, make love, and shriek his mind,
By throngs of strangers undisprivacied.
He makes his life a public gallery,
Nor feels himself till what he feels comes back
In manifold reflection from without;
While we, each pore alert with consciousness,
Hide our best selves as we had stolen them,
And each bystander a detective were,
Keen-eyed for every chink of undisguise.

v

So, musing o'er the problem which was best, —
A life wide-windowed, shining all abroad,
Or curtains drawn to shield from sight profane
The rites we pay to the mysterious I, —
With outward senses furloughed and head bowed
I followed some fine instinct in my feet,
Till, to unbend me from the loom of thought,
Looking up suddenly, I found mine eyes
Confronted with the minster's vast repose.
Silent and gray as forest-leaguered cliff
Left inland by the ocean's slow retreat,
That hears afar the breeze-borne rote and longs,
Remembering shocks of surf that clomb and fell,
Spume-sliding down the baffled decuman,
It rose before me, patiently remote
From the great tides of life it breasted once,
Hearing the noise of men as in a dream.
I stood before the triple northern port,
Where dedicated shapes of saints and kings,
Stern faces bleared with immemorial watch,
Looked down benignly grave and seemed to say,
Ye come and go incessant ; we remain
Safe in the hallowed quiets of the past ;
Be reverent, ye who flit and are forgot,
Of faith so nobly realized as this.
I seem to have heard it said by learnèd folk
Who drench you with æsthetics till you feel
As if all beauty were a ghastly bore,
The faucet to let loose a wash of words,
That Gothic is not Grecian, therefore worse ;
But, being convinced by much experiment
How little inventiveness there is in man,

Grave copier of copies, I give thanks
For a new relish, careless to inquire
My pleasure's pedigree, if so it please,
Nobly, I mean, nor renegade to art.
The Grecian gluts me with its perfectness,
Unanswerable as Euclid, self-contained,
The one thing finished in this hasty world,
Forever finished, though the barbarous pit,
Fanatical on hearsay, stamp and shout
As if a miracle could be encored.
But ah! this other, this that never ends,
Still climbing, luring fancy still to climb,
As full of morals half-divined as life,
Graceful, grotesque, with ever new surprise
Of hazardous caprices sure to please,
Heavy as nightmare, airy-light as fern,
Imagination's very self in stone!
With one long sigh of infinite release
From pedantries past, present, or to come,
I looked, and owned myself a happy Goth.
Your blood is mine, ye architects of dream,
Builders of aspiration incomplete,
So more consummate, souls self-confident,
Who felt your own thought worthy of record
In monumental pomp! No Grecian drop
Rebukes these veins that leap with kindred thrill,
After long exile, to the mother tongue.

Ovid in Pontus, puling for his Rome
Of men invirile and disnatured dames
That poison sucked from the Attic bloom decayed,
Shrank with a shudder from the blue-eyed race

Whose force rough-handed should renew the world,
And from the dregs of Romulus express
Such wine as Dante poured, or he who blew
Roland's vain blast, or sang the Campeador
In verse that clanks like armor in the charge,
Homeric juice, though brimmed in Odin's horn.
And they could build, if not the columned fane
That from the height gleamed seaward many-hued,
Something more friendly with their ruder skies:
The gray spire, molten now in driving mist,
Now lulled with the incommunicable blue;
The carvings touched to meaning new with snow,
Or commented with fleeting grace of shade;
The statues, motley as man's memory,
Partial as that, so mixed of true and false,
History and legend meeting with a kiss
Across this bound-mark where their realms confine;
The painted windows, freaking gloom with glow,
Dusking the sunshine which they seem to cheer,
Meet symbol of the senses and the soul,
And the whole pile, grim with the Northman's thought
Of life and death, and doom, life's equal fee, —
These were before me: and I gazed abashed,
Child of an age that lectures, not creates,
Plastering our swallow-nests on the awful Past,
And twittering round the work of larger men,
As we had builded what we but deface.
Far up the great bells wallowed in delight,
Tossing their clangors o'er the heedless town,
To call the worshippers who never came,
Or women mostly, in loath twos and threes.
I entered, reverent of whatever shrine

Guards piety and solace for my kind
Or gives the soul a moment's truce of God,
And shared decorous in the ancient rite
My sterner fathers held idolatrous.
The service over, I was tranced in thought :
Solemn the deepening vaults, and most to me,
Fresh from the fragile realm of deal and paint,
Or brick mock-pious with a marble front ;
Solemn the lift of high-embowered roof,
The clustered stems that spread in boughs disleaved,
Through which the organ blew a dream of storm,
Though not more potent to sublime with awe
And shut the heart up in tranquillity,
Than aisles to me familiar that o'erarch
The conscious silences of brooding woods,
Centurial shadows, cloisters of the elk :
Yet here was sense of undefined regret,
Irreparable loss, uncertain what :
Was all this grandeur but anachronism,
A shell divorced of its informing life,
Where the priest housed him like a hermit-crab,
An alien to that faith of elder days
That gathered round it this fair shape of stone ?
Is old Religion but a spectre now,
Haunting the solitude of darkened minds,
Mocked out of memory by the sceptic day ?
Is there no corner safe from peeping Doubt,
Since Gutenberg made thought cosmopolite
And stretched electric threads from mind to mind ?
Nay, did Faith build this wonder ? or did Fear,
That makes a fetish and misnames it God
(Blockish or metaphysic, matters not),

Contrive this coop to shut its tyrant in,
Appeased with playthings, that he might not harm?

I turned and saw a beldame on her knees;
With eyes astray, she told mechanic beads
Before some shrine of saintly womanhood,
Bribed intercessor with the far-off Judge:
Such my first thought, by kindlier soon rebuked,
Pleading for whatsoever touches life
With upward impulse: be He nowhere else,
God is in all that liberates and lifts,
In all that humbles, sweetens, and consoles:
Blessëd the natures shored on every side
With landmarks of hereditary thought!
Thrice happy they that wander not life long.
Beyond near succor of the household faith,
The guarded fold that shelters, not confines!
Their steps find patience in familiar paths,
Printed with hope by loved feet gone before
Of parent, child, or lover, glorified
By simple magic of dividing Time.
My lids were moistened as the woman knelt,
And — was it will, or some vibration faint
Of sacred Nature, deeper than the will? —
My heart occultly felt itself in hers,
Through mutual intercession gently leagued.

Or was it not mere sympathy of brain?
A sweetness intellectually conceived
In simpler creeds to me impossible?
A juggle of that pity for ourselves
In others, which puts on such pretty masks

And snares self-love with bait of charity?
Something of all it might be, or of none:
Yet for a moment I was snatched away
And had the evidence of things not seen;
For one rapt moment; then it all came back,
This age that blots out life with question-marks,
This nineteenth century with its knife and glass
That make thought physical, and thrust far off
The Heaven, so neighborly with man of old,
To voids sparse-sown with alienated stars.

'T is irrecoverable, that ancient faith,
Homely and wholesome, suited to the time,
With rod or candy for child-minded men:
No theologic tube, with lens on lens
Of syllogism transparent, brings it near, —
At best resolving some new nebula,
Or blurring some fixed star of hope to mist.
Science was Faith once; Faith were Science now,
Would she but lay her bow and arrows by
And arm her with the weapons of the time.
Nothing that keeps thought out is safe from thought.
For there's no virgin-fort but self-respect,
And Truth defensive hath lost hold on God.
Shall we treat Him as if He were a child
That knew not His own purpose? nor dare trust
The Rock of Ages to their chemic tests,
Lest some day the all-sustaining base divine
Should fail from under us, dissolved in gas?
The arméd eye that with a glance discerns
In a dry blood-speck between ox and man,
Stares helpless at this miracle called life,

This shaping potency behind the egg,
This circulation swift of deity,
Where suns and systems inconspicuous float
As the poor blood-disks in our mortal veins.
Each age must worship its own thought of God,
More or less earthy, clarifying still
With subsidence continuous of the dregs;
Nor saint nor sage could fix immutably
The fluent image of the unstable Best,
Still changing in their very hands that wrought:
To-day's eternal truth To-morrow proved
Frail as frost-landscapes on a window-pane.
Meanwhile Thou smiledst, inaccessible,
At Thought's own substance made a cage for
          Thought,
And Truth locked fast with her own master-key;
Nor didst Thou reck what image man might make
Of his own shadow on the flowing world;
The climbing instinct was enough for Thee.
Or wast Thou, then, an ebbing tide that left
Strewn with dead miracle those eldest shores,
For men to dry, and dryly lecture on,
Thyself thenceforth incapable of flood?
Idle who hopes with prophets to be snatched
By virtue in their mantles left below;
Shall the soul live on other men's report,
Herself a pleasing fable of herself?
Man cannot be God's outlaw if he would,
Nor so abscond him in the caves of sense
But Nature still shall search some crevice out
With messages of splendor from that Source
Which, dive he, soar he, baffles still and lures.

This life were brutish did we not sometimes
Have intimation clear of wider scope,
Hints of occasion infinite, to keep
The soul alert with noble discontent
And onward yearnings of unstilled desire;
Fruitless, except we now and then divined
A mystery of Purpose, gleaming through
The secular confusions of the world,
Whose will we darkly accomplish, doing ours.
No man can think nor in himself perceive,
Sometimes at waking, in the street sometimes,
Or on the hillside, always unforewarned,
A grace of being, finer than himself,
That beckons and is gone, — a larger life
Upon his own impinging, with swift glimpse
Of spacious circles luminous with mind,
To which the ethereal substance of his own
Seems but gross cloud to make that visible,
Touched to a sudden glory round the edge.
Who that hath known these visitations fleet
Would strive to make them trite and ritual?
I, that still pray at morning and at eve,
Loving those roots that feed us from the past,
And prizing more than Plato things I learned
At that best academe, a mother's knee,
Thrice in my life perhaps have truly prayed,
Thrice, stirred below my conscious self, have felt
That perfect disenthralment which is God;
Nor know I which to hold worst enemy,
Him who on speculation's windy waste
Would turn me loose, stript of the raiment warm
By Faith contrived against our nakedness,

Or him who, cruel-kind, would fain obscure,
With painted saints and paraphrase of God,
The soul's east-window of divine surprise.
Where others worship I but look and long;
For, though not recreant to my fathers' faith,
Its forms to me are weariness, and most
That drony vacuum of compulsory prayer,
Still pumping phrases for the Ineffable,
Though all the valves of memory gasp and wheeze.
Words that have drawn transcendent meanings up
From the best passion of all bygone time,
Steeped through with tears of triumph and remorse,
Sweet with all sainthood, cleansed in martyr-fires,
Can they, so consecrate and so inspired,
By repetition wane to vexing wind?
Alas! we cannot draw habitual breath
In the thin air of life's supremer heights,
We cannot make each meal a sacrament,
Nor with our tailors be disbodied souls, —
We men, too conscious of earth's comedy,
Who see two sides, with our posed selves debate,
And only for great stakes can be sublime!
Let us be thankful when, as I do here,
We can read Bethel on a pile of stones,
And, seeing where God *has* been, trust in Him.

Brave Peter Fischer there in Nuremberg,
Moulding Saint Sebald's miracles in bronze,
Put saint and stander-by in that quaint garb
Familiar to him in his daily walk,
Not doubting God could grant a miracle
Then and in Nuremberg, if so He would;

But never artist for three hundred years
Hath dared the contradiction ludicrous
Of supernatural in modern clothes.
Perhaps the deeper faith that is to come
Will see God rather in the strenuous doubt,
Than in the creed held as an infant's hand
Holds purposeless whatso is placed therein.

Say it is drift, not progress, none the less,
With the old sextant of the fathers' creed,
We shape our courses by new-risen stars,
And, still lip-loyal to what once was truth,
Smuggle new meanings under ancient names,
Unconscious perverts of the Jesuit, Time.
Change is the mask that all Continuance wears
To keep us youngsters harmlessly amused;
Meanwhile some ailing or more watchful child,
Sitting apart, sees the old eyes gleam out,
Stern, and yet soft with humorous pity too.
Whilere, men burnt men for a doubtful point,
As if the mind were quenchable with fire,
And Faith danced round them with her war-paint
        on,
Devoutly savage as an Iroquois;
Now Calvin and Servetus at one board
Snuff in grave sympathy a milder roast,
And o'er their claret settle Comte unread.
Fagot and stake were desperately sincere:
Our cooler martyrdoms are done in types;
And flames that shine in controversial eyes
Burn out no brains but his who kindles them.
This is no age to get cathedrals built:

Did God, then, wait for one in Bethlehem?
Worst is not yet : lo, where his coming looms,
Of Earth's anarchic children latest born,
Democracy, a Titan who hath learned
To laugh at Jove's old-fashioned thunderbolts, —
Could he not also forge them, if he would?
He, better skilled, with solvents merciless,
Loosened in air and borne on every wind,
Saps unperceived : the calm Olympian height
Of ancient order feels its bases yield,
And pale gods glance for help to gods as pale.
What will be left of good or worshipful,
Of spiritual secrets, mysteries,
Of fair religion's guarded heritage,
Heirlooms of soul, passed downward unprofaned
From eldest Ind ? This Western giant coarse,
Scorning refinements which he lacks himself,
Loves not nor heeds the ancestral hierarchies,
Each rank dependent on the next above
In orderly gradation fixed as fate.
King by mere manhood, nor allowing aught
Of holier unction than the sweat of toil ;
In his own strength sufficient ; called to solve,
On the rough edges of society,
Problems long sacred to the choicer few,
And improvise what elsewhere men receive
As gifts of deity ; tough foundling reared
Where every man's his own Melchisedek,
How make him reverent of a King of kings ?
Or Judge self-made, executor of laws
By him not first discussed and voted on ?
For him no tree of knowledge is forbid,

Or sweeter if forbid. How save the ark,
Or holy of holies, unprofaned a day
From his unscrupulous curiosity
That handles everything as if to buy,
Tossing aside what fabrics delicate
Suit not the rough-and-tumble of his ways?
What hope for those fine-nerved humanities
That made earth gracious once with gentler arts,
Now the rude hands have caught the trick of thought
And claim an equal suffrage with the brain?

The born disciple of an elder time
(To me sufficient, friendlier than the new),
Who in my blood feel motions of the Past,
I thank benignant Nature most for this, —
A force of sympathy, or call it lack
Of character firm-planted, loosing me
From the pent chamber of habitual self
To dwell enlarged in alien modes of thought,
Haply distasteful, wholesomer for that,
And through imagination to possess,
As they were mine, the lives of other men.
This growth original of virgin soil,
By fascination felt in opposites,
Pleases and shocks, entices and perturbs.
In this brown-fisted rough, this shirt-sleeved Cid,
This backwoods Charlemagne of empires new,
Whose blundering heel instinctively finds out
The goutier foot of speechless dignities,
Who, meeting Cæsar's self, would slap his back,
Call him " Old Horse," and challenge to a drink,
My lungs draw braver air, my breast dilates

With ampler manhood, and I front both worlds,
Of sense and spirit, as my natural fiefs,
To shape and then reshape them as I will.
It was the first man's charter; why not mine?
How forfeit? when deposed in other hands?

Thou shudder'st, Ovid? Dost in him forebode
A new avatar of the large-limbed Goth,
To break, or seem to break, tradition's clue,
And chase to dreamland back thy gods dethroned?
I think man's soul dwells nearer to the east,
Nearer to morning's fountains than the sun;
Herself the source whence all tradition sprang,
Herself at once both labyrinth and clue.
The miracle fades out of history,
But faith and wonder and the primal earth
Are born into the world with every child.
Shall this self-maker with the prying eyes,
This creature disenchanted of respect
By the New World's new fiend, Publicity,
Whose testing thumb leaves everywhere its smutch,
Not one day feel within himself the need
Of loyalty to better than himself,
That shall ennoble him with the upward look?
Shall he not catch the Voice that wanders earth,
With spiritual summons, dreamed or heard,
As sometimes, just ere sleep seals up the sense,
We hear our mother call from deeps of Time,
And, waking, find it vision, — none the less
The benediction bides, old skies return,
And that unreal thing, preëminent,
Makes air and dream of all we see and feel?
Shall he divine no strength unmade of votes,

Inward, impregnable, found soon as sought,
Not cognizable of sense, o'er sense supreme?
Else were he desolate as none before.
His holy places may not be of stone,
Nor made with hands, yet fairer far than aught
By artist feigned or pious ardor reared,
Fit altars for who guards inviolate
God's chosen seat, the sacred form of man.
Doubtless his church will be no hospital
For superannuate forms and mumping shams,
No parlor where men issue policies
Of life-assurance on the Eternal Mind,
Nor his religion but an ambulance
To fetch life's wounded and malingerers in,
Scorned by the strong; yet he, unconscious heir
To the influence sweet of Athens and of Rome,
And old Judæa's gift of secret fire,
Spite of himself shall surely learn to know
And worship some ideal of himself,
Some divine thing, large-hearted, brotherly,
Not nice in trifles, a soft creditor,
Pleased with his world, and hating only cant.
And, if his Church be doubtful, it is sure
That, in a world, made for whatever else,
Not made for mere enjoyment, in a world
Of toil but half-requited, or, at best,
Paid in some futile currency of breath,
A world of incompleteness, sorrow swift
And consolation laggard, whatsoe'er
The form of building or the creed professed,
The Cross, bold type of shame to homage turned,
Of an unfinished life that sways the world,
Shall tower as sovereign emblem over all.

The kobold Thought moves with us when we shift
Our dwelling to escape him ; perched aloft
On the first load of household-stuff he went ;
For, where the mind goes, goes old furniture.
I, who to Chartres came to feed my eye
And give to Fancy one clear holiday,
Scarce saw the minster for the thoughts it stirred
Buzzing o'er past and future with vain quest.
Here once there stood a homely wooden church,
Which slow devotion nobly changed for this
That echoes vaguely to my modern steps.
By suffrage universal it was built,
As practised then, for all the country came
From far as Rouen, to give votes for God,
Each vote a block of stone securely laid
Obedient to the master's deep-mused plan.
Will what our ballots rear, responsible
To no grave forethought, stand so long as this ?
Delight like this the eye of after days
Brightening with pride that here, at least, were men
Who meant and did the noblest thing they knew ?
Can our religion cope with deeds like this ?
We, too, build Gothic contract-shams, because
Our deacons have discovered that it pays,
And pews sell better under vaulted roofs
Of plaster painted like an Indian squaw.
Shall not that Western Goth, of whom we spoke,
So fiercely practical, so keen of eye,
Find out, some day, that nothing pays but God,
Served whether on the smoke-shut battle-field,
In work obscure done honestly, or vote
For truth unpopular, or faith maintained

To ruinous convictions, or good deeds
Wrought for good's sake, mindless of heaven or
    hell ?
Shall he not learn that all prosperity,
Whose bases stretch not deeper than the sense,
Is but a trick of this world's atmosphere,
A desert-born mirage of spire and dome,
Or find too late, the Past's long lesson missed,
That dust the prophets shake from off their feet
Grows heavy to drag down both tower and wall ?
I know not ; but, sustained by sure belief
That man still rises level with the height
Of noblest opportunities, or makes
Such, if the time supply not, I can wait.
I gaze round on the windows, pride of France,
Each the bright gift of some mechanic guild
Who loved their city and thought gold well spent
To make her beautiful with piety ;
I pause, transfigured by some stripe of bloom,
And my mind throngs with shining auguries,
Circle on circle, bright as seraphim,
With golden trumpets, silent, that await
The signal to blow news of good to men.

Then the revulsion came that always comes
After these dizzy elations of the mind :
And with a passionate pang of doubt I cried,
" O mountain-born, sweet with snow-filtered air
From uncontaminate wells of ether drawn
And never-broken secrecies of sky,
Freedom, with anguish won, misprized till lost,
They keep thee not who from thy sacred eyes

v

Catch the consuming lust of sensual good
And the brute's license of unfettered will.
Far from the popular shout and venal breath
Of Cleon blowing the mob's baser mind
To bubbles of wind-piloted conceit,
Thou shrinkest, gathering up thy skirts, to hide
In fortresses of solitary thought
And private virtue strong in self-restraint.
Must we too forfeit thee misunderstood,
Content with names, nor inly wise to know
That best things perish of their own excess,
And quality o'er-driven becomes defect?
Nay, is it thou indeed that we have glimpsed,
Or rather such illusion as of old
Through Athens glided menadlike, and Rome,
A shape of vapor, mother of vain dreams
And mutinous traditions, specious plea
Of the glaived tyrant and long-memoried priest?"

I walked forth saddened; for all thought is sad,
And leaves a bitterish savor in the brain,
Tonic, it may be, not delectable;
And turned, reluctant, for a parting look
At those old weather-pitted images
Of bygone struggle, now so sternly calm.
About their shoulders sparrows had built nests,
And fluttered, chirping, from gray perch to perch,
Now on a mitre poising, now a crown,
Irreverently happy. While I thought
How confident they were, what careless hearts
Flew on those lightsome wings and shared the
　　　sun,

A larger shadow crossed; and looking up,
I saw where, nesting in the hoary towers,
The sparrow-hawk slid forth on noiseless air,
With sidelong head that watched the joy below,
Grim Norman baron o'er this clan of Kelts.
Enduring Nature, force conservative,
Indifferent to our noisy whims! Men prate
Of all heads to an equal grade cashiered
On level with the dullest, and expect
(Sick of no worse distemper than themselves)
A wondrous cure-all in equality;
They reason that To-morrow must be wise
Because To-day was not, nor Yesterday,
As if good days were shapen of themselves,
Not of the very lifeblood of men's souls;
Meanwhile, long-suffering, imperturbable,
Thou quietly complet'st thy syllogism,
And from the premise sparrow here below
Draw'st sure conclusion of the hawk above,
Pleased with the soft-billed songster, pleased no
        less
With the fierce beak of natures aquiline.

Thou beautiful Old Time, now hid away
In the Past's valley of Avilion,
Haply, like Arthur, till thy wound be healed,
Then to reclaim the sword and crown again!
Thrice beautiful to us; perchance less fair
To who possessed thee, as a mountain seems
To dwellers round its bases but a heap
Of barren obstacle that lairs the storm
And the avalanche's silent bolt holds back

Leashed with a hair,—meanwhile some far-off
    clown,
Hereditary delver of the plain,
Sees it an unmoved vision of repose,
Nest of the morning, and conjectures there
The dance of streams to idle shepherds' pipes,
And fairer habitations softly hung
On breezy slopes, or hid in valleys cool,
For happier men. No mortal ever dreams
That the scant isthmus he encamps upon
Between two oceans, one, the Stormy, passed,
And one, the Peaceful, yet to venture on,
Has been that future whereto prophets yearned
For the fulfilment of Earth's cheated hope,
Shall be that past which nerveless poets moan
As the lost opportunity of song.

O Power, more near my life than life itself
(Or what seems life to us in sense immured),
Even as the roots, shut in the darksome earth,
Share in the tree-top's joyance, and conceive
Of sunshine and wide air and wingèd things
By sympathy of nature, so do I
Have evidence of Thee so far above,
Yet in and of me! Rather Thou the root
Invisibly sustaining, hid in light,
Not darkness, or in darkness made by us.
If sometimes I must hear good men debate
Of other witness of Thyself than Thou,
As if there needed any help of ours
To nurse Thy flickering life, that else must cease,
Blown out, as 't were a candle, by men's breath,

My soul shall not be taken in their snare,
To change her inward surety for their doubt
Muffled from sight in formal robes of proof:
While she can only feel herself through Thee,
I fear not Thy withdrawal; more I fear,
Seeing, to know Thee not, hoodwinked with dreams
Of signs and wonders, while, unnoticed, Thou,
Walking Thy garden still, commun'st with men,
Missed in the commonplace of miracle.

THREE MEMORIAL POEMS

" Coscienza fusca
O della propria o dell' altrui vergogna
Pur sentirà la tua parola brusca."

If I let fall a word of bitter mirth
When public shames more shameful pardon won,
Some have misjudged me, and my service done,
If small, yet faithful, deemed of little worth:
Through veins that drew their life from Western earth
Two hundred years and more my blood hath run
In no polluted course from sire to son;
And thus was I predestined ere my birth
To love the soil wherewith my fibres own
Instinctive sympathies; yet love it so
As honor would, nor lightly to dethrone
Judgment, the stamp of manhood, nor forego
The son's right to a mother dearer grown
With growing knowledge and more chaste than snow.

To

E. L. GODKIN

IN CORDIAL ACKNOWLEDGMENT OF HIS EMINENT SERVICE IN
HEIGHTENING AND PURIFYING THE TONE OF
OUR POLITICAL THOUGHT

These Three Poems

ARE DEDICATED

*** Readers, it is hoped, will remember that, by his Ode at the Harvard Commemoration, the author had precluded himself from many of the natural outlets of thought and feeling common to such occasions as are celebrated in these poems.

ODE

READ AT THE ONE HUNDREDTH ANNIVERSARY OF
THE FIGHT AT CONCORD BRIDGE

19TH APRIL, 1875

I

Who cometh over the hills,
Her garments with morning sweet,
The dance of a thousand rills
Making music before her feet?
Her presence freshens the air;
Sunshine steals light from her face;
The leaden footstep of Care
Leaps to the tune of her pace,
Fairness of all that is fair,
Grace at the heart of all grace,
Sweetener of hut and of hall,
Bringer of life out of naught,
Freedom, oh, fairest of all
The daughters of Time and Thought!

II

She cometh, cometh to-day:
Hark! hear ye not her tread,
Sending a thrill through your clay,
Under the sod there, ye dead,
Her nurslings and champions?

Do ye not hear, as she comes,
The bay of the deep-mouthed guns,
The gathering rote of the drums?
The bells that called ye to prayer,
How wildly they clamor on her,
Crying, "She cometh! prepare
Her to praise and her to honor,
That a hundred years ago
Scattered here in blood and tears
Potent seeds wherefrom should grow
Gladness for a hundred years!"

III

Tell me, young men, have ye seen,
Creature of diviner mien
For true hearts to long and cry for,
Manly hearts to live and die for?
What hath she that others want?
Brows that all endearments haunt,
Eyes that make it sweet to dare,
Smiles that cheer untimely death,
Looks that fortify despair,
Tones more brave than trumpet's breath;
Tell me, maidens, have ye known
Household charm more sweetly rare,
Grace of woman ampler blown,
Modesty more debonair,
Younger heart with wit full grown?
Oh for an hour of my prime,
The pulse of my hotter years,
That I might praise her in rhyme
Would tingle your eyelids to tears,

Our sweetness, our strength, and our star,
Our hope, our joy, and our trust,
Who lifted us out of the dust,
And made us whatever we are!

IV

Whiter than moonshine upon snow
Her raiment is, but round the hem
Crimson stained; and, as to and fro
Her sandals flash, we see on them,
And on her instep veined with blue,
Flecks of crimson, on those fair feet,
High-arched, Diana-like, and fleet,
Fit for no grosser stain than dew:
Oh, call them rather chrisms than stains,
Sacred and from heroic veins!
For, in the glory-guarded pass,
Her haughty and far-shining head
She bowed to shrive Leonidas
With his imperishable dead;
Her, too, Morgarten saw,
Where the Swiss lion fleshed his icy paw;
She followed Cromwell's quenchless star
Where the grim Puritan tread
Shook Marston, Naseby, and Dunbar:
Yea, on her feet are dearer dyes
Yet fresh, nor looked on with untearful eyes.

V

Our fathers found her in the woods
Where Nature meditates and broods,

The seeds of unexampled things
Which Time to consummation brings
Through life and death and man's unstable moods;
They met her here, not recognized,
A sylvan huntress clothed in furs,
To whose chaste wants her bow sufficed,
Nor dreamed what destinies were hers:
She taught them bee-like to create
Their simpler forms of Church and State;
She taught them to endue
The past with other functions than it knew,
And turn in channels strange the uncertain stream
  of Fate;
Better than all, she fenced them in their need
With iron-handed Duty's sternest creed,
'Gainst Self's lean wolf that ravens word and deed.

VI

Why cometh she hither to-day
To this low village of the plain
Far from the Present's loud highway,
From Trade's cool heart and seething brain?
Why cometh she? She was not far away.
Since the soul touched it, not in vain,
With pathos of immortal gain,
'T is here her fondest memories stay.
She loves yon pine-bemurmured ridge
Where now our broad-browed poet sleeps,
Dear to both Englands; near him he
Who wore the ring of Canace;
But most her heart to rapture leaps

Where stood that era-parting bridge,
O'er which, with footfall still as dew,
The Old Time passed into the New;
Where, as your stealthy river creeps,
He whispers to his listening weeds
Tales of sublimest homespun deeds.
Here English law and English thought
'Gainst the self-will of England fought;
And here were men (coequal with their fate),
Who did great things, unconscious they were great.
They dreamed not what a die was cast
With that first answering shot; what then?
There was their duty; they were men
Schooled the soul's inward gospel to obey,
Though leading to the lion's den.
They felt the habit-hallowed world give way
Beneath their lives, and on went they,
Unhappy who was last.
When Buttrick gave the word,
That awful idol of the unchallenged Past,
Strong in their love, and in their lineage strong,
Fell crashing: if they heard it not,
Yet the earth heard,
Nor ever hath forgot,
As on from startled throne to throne,
Where Superstition sate or conscious Wrong,
A shudder ran of some dread birth unknown.
Thrice venerable spot!
River more fateful than the Rubicon!
O'er those red planks, to snatch her diadem,
Man's Hope, star-girdled, sprang with them,
And over ways untried the feet of Doom strode on.

VII

Think you these felt no charms
In their gray homesteads and embowered farms?
In household faces waiting at the door
Their evening step should lighten up no more?
In fields their boyish feet had known?
In trees their fathers' hands had set,
And which with them had grown,
Widening each year their leafy coronet?
Felt they no pang of passionate regret
For those unsolid goods that seem so much our own?
These things are dear to every man that lives,
And life prized more for what it lends than gives.
Yea, many a tie, through iteration sweet,
Strove to detain their fatal feet;
And yet the enduring half they chose,
Whose choice decides a man life's slave or king,
The invisible things of God before the seen and
        known:
Therefore their memory inspiration blows
With echoes gathering on from zone to zone;
For manhood is the one immortal thing
Beneath Time's changeful sky,
And, where it lightened once, from age to age,
Men come to learn, in grateful pilgrimage,
That length of days is knowing when to die.

VIII

What marvellous change of things and men!
She, a world-wandering orphan then,
So mighty now! Those are her streams

That whirl the myriad, myriad wheels
Of all that does, and all that dreams,
Of all that thinks, and all that feels,
Through spaces stretched from sea to sea;
By idle tongues and busy brains,
By who doth right, and who refrains,
Hers are our losses and our gains;
Our maker and our victim she.

IX

Maiden half mortal, half divine,
We triumphed in thy coming; to the brinks
Our hearts were filled with pride's tumultuous wine;
Better to-day who rather feels than thinks.
Yet will some graver thoughts intrude,
And cares of sterner mood;
They won thee: who shall keep thee? From the
     deeps
Where discrowned empires o'er their ruins brood,
And many a thwarted hope wrings its weak hands
     and weeps,
I hear the voice as of a mighty wind
From all heaven's caverns rushing unconfined,
" I, Freedom, dwell with Knowledge: I abide
With men whom dust of faction cannot blind
To the slow tracings of the Eternal Mind;
With men by culture trained and fortified,
Who bitter duty to sweet lusts prefer,
Fearless to counsel and obey.
Conscience my sceptre is, and law my sword,
Not to be drawn in passion or in play,
But terrible to punish and deter;

Implacable as God's word, .
Like it, a shepherd's crook to them that blindly err.
Your firm-pulsed sires, my martyrs and my saints,
Offshoots of that one stock whose patient sense
Hath known to mingle flux with permanence,
Rated my chaste denials and restraints
Above the moment's dear-paid paradise:
Beware lest, shifting with Time's gradual creep,
The light that guided shine into your eyes.
The envious Powers of ill nor wink nor sleep:
Be therefore timely wise,
Nor laugh when this one steals, and that one lies,
As if your luck could cheat those sleepless spies,
Till the deaf Fury comes your house to sweep!"
I hear the voice, and unaffrighted bow;
Ye shall not be prophetic now,
Heralds of ill, that darkening fly
Between my vision and the rainbowed sky,
Or on the left your hoarse forebodings croak
From many a blasted bough
On Yggdrasil's storm-sinewed oak,
That once was green, Hope of the West, as thou:
Yet pardon if I tremble while I boast;
For I have loved as those who pardon most.

X

Away, ungrateful doubt, away!
At least she is our own to-day.
Break into rapture, my song,
Verses, leap forth in the sun,
Bearing the joyance along
Like a train of fire as ye run!

Pause not for choosing of words,
Let them but blossom and sing
Blithe as the orchards and birds
With the new coming of spring!
Dance in your jollity, bells;
Shout, cannon; cease not, ye drums;
Answer, ye hillside and dells;
Bow, all ye people! She comes,
Radiant, calm-fronted, as when
She hallowed that April day.
Stay with us! Yes, thou shalt stay,
Softener and strengthener of men,
Freedom, not won by the vain,
Not to be courted in play,
Not to be kept without pain.
Stay with us! Yes, thou wilt stay,
Handmaid and mistress of all,
Kindler of deed and of thought,
Thou that to hut and to hall
Equal deliverance brought!
Souls of her martyrs, draw near,
Touch our dull lips with your fire,
That we may praise without fear
Her our delight, our desire,
Our faith's inextinguishable star,
Our hope, our remembrance, our trust,
Our present, our past, our to be,
Who will mingle her life with our dust
And makes us deserve to be free!

V

UNDER THE OLD ELM

POEM READ AT CAMBRIDGE ON THE HUNDREDTH ANNI-
VERSARY OF WASHINGTON'S TAKING COMMAND OF
THE AMERICAN ARMY, 3D JULY, 1775

I

1

WORDS pass as wind, but where great deeds were
    done
A power abides transfused from sire to son :
The boy feels deeper meanings thrill his ear,
That tingling through his pulse lifelong shall run,
With sure impulsion to keep honor clear,
When, pointing down, his father whispers, " Here,
Here, where we stand, stood he, the purely great,
Whose soul no siren passion could unsphere,
Then nameless, now a power and mixed with fate."
Historic town, thou holdest sacred dust,
Once known to men as pious, learnëd, just,
And one memorial pile that dares to last ;
But Memory greets with reverential kiss
No spot in all thy circuit sweet as this,
Touched by that modest glory as it past,
O'er which yon elm hath piously displayed
These hundred years its monumental shade.

The Washington Elm

II

Of our swift passage through this scenery
Of life and death, more durable than we,
What landmark so congenial as a tree
Repeating its green legend every spring,
And, with a yearly ring,
Recording the fair seasons as they flee,
Type of our brief but still-renewed mortality?
We fall as leaves: the immortal trunk remains,
Builded with costly juice of hearts and brains
Gone to the mould now, whither all that be
Vanish returnless, yet are procreant still
In human lives to come of good or ill,
And feed unseen the roots of Destiny.

II

I

Men's monuments, grown old, forget their names
They should eternize, but the place
Where shining souls have passed imbibes a grace
Beyond mere earth; some sweetness of their fames
Leaves in the soil its unextinguished trace,
Pungent, pathetic, sad with nobler aims,
That penetrates our lives and heightens them or
        shames.
This insubstantial world and fleet
Seems solid for a moment when we stand
On dust ennobled by heroic feet
Once mighty to sustain a tottering land,
And mighty still such burthen to upbear,

Nor doomed to tread the path of things that merely
      were :
Our sense, refined with virtue of the spot,
Across the mists of Lethe's sleepy stream
Recalls him, the sole chief without a blot,
No more a pallid image and a dream,
But as he dwelt with men decorously supreme.

II

Our grosser minds need this terrestrial hint
To raise long-buried days from tombs of print :
" Here stood he," softly we repeat,
And lo, the statue shrined and still
In that gray minster-front we call the Past,
Feels in its frozen veins our pulses thrill,
Breathes living air and mocks at Death's deceit.
It warms, it stirs, comes down to us at last,
Its features human with familiar light,
A man, beyond the historian's art to kill,
Or sculptor's to efface with patient chisel-blight.

III

Sure the dumb earth hath memory, nor for naught
Was Fancy given, on whose enchanted loom
Present and Past commingle, fruit and bloom
Of one fair bough, inseparably wrought
Into the seamless tapestry of thought.
So charmed, with undeluded eye we see
In history's fragmentary tale
Bright clues of continuity,
Learn that high natures over Time prevail,
And feel ourselves a link in that entail
That binds all ages past with all that are to be.

III

I

Beneath our consecrated elm
A century ago he stood,
Famed vaguely for that old fight in the wood
Whose red surge sought, but could not overwhelm
The life foredoomed to wield our rough-hewn helm:
From colleges, where now the gown
To arms had yielded, from the town,
Our rude self-summoned levies flocked to see
The new-come chiefs and wonder which was he.
No need to question long; close-lipped and tall,
Long trained in murder-brooding forests lone
To bridle others' clamors and his own,
Firmly erect, he towered above them all,
The incarnate discipline that was to free
With iron curb that armed democracy.

II

A motley rout was that which came to stare,
In raiment tanned by years of sun and storm,
Of every shape that was not uniform,
Dotted with regimentals here and there;
An army all of captains, used to pray
And stiff in fight, but serious drill's despair,
Skilled to debate their orders, not obey;
Deacons were there, selectmen, men of note
In half-tamed hamlets ambushed round with woods,
Ready to settle Freewill by a vote,

But largely liberal to its private moods;
Prompt to assert by manners, voice, or pen,
Or ruder arms, their rights as Englishmen,
Nor much fastidious as to how and when:
Yet seasoned stuff and fittest to create
A thought-staid army or a lasting state:
Haughty they said he was, at first; severe;
But owned, as all men own, the steady hand
Upon the bridle, patient to command,
Prized, as all prize, the justice pure from fear,
And learned to honor first, then love him, then re-
      vere.
Such power there is in clear-eyed self-restraint
And purpose clean as light from every selfish taint.

III

Musing beneath the legendary tree,
The years between furl off: I seem to see
The sun-flecks, shaken the stirred foliage through,
Dapple with gold his sober buff and blue
And weave prophetic aureoles round the head
That shines our beacon now nor darkens with the
      dead.
O man of silent mood,
A stranger among strangers then,
How art thou since renowned the Great, the Good,
Familiar as the day in all the homes of men!
The wingèd years, that winnow praise and blame,
Blow many names out: they but fan to flame
The self-renewing splendors of thy fame.

IV

I

How many subtlest influences unite,
With spiritual touch of joy or pain,
Invisible as air and soft as light,
To body forth that image of the brain
We call our Country, visionary shape,
Loved more than woman, fuller of fire than wine,
Whose charm can none define,
Nor any, though he flee it, can escape!
All party-colored threads the weaver Time
Sets in his web, now trivial, now sublime,
All memories, all forebodings, hopes and fears,
Mountain and river, forest, prairie, sea,
A hill, a rock, a homestead, field, or tree,
The casual gleanings of unreckoned years,
Take goddess-shape at last and there is She,
Old at our birth, new as the springing hours,
Shrine of our weakness, fortress of our powers,
Consoler, kindler, peerless 'mid her peers,
A force that 'neath our conscious being stirs,
A life to give ours permanence, when we
Are borne to mingle our poor earth with hers,
And all this glowing world goes with us on our biers.

II

Nations are long results, by ruder ways
Gathering the might that warrants length of days;
They may be pieced of half-reluctant shares
Welded by hammer-strokes of broad-brained kings,

Or from a doughty people grow, the heirs
Of wise traditions widening cautious rings;
At best they are computable things,
A strength behind us making us feel bold
In right, or, as may chance, in wrong;
Whose force by figures may be summed and told,
So many soldiers, ships, and dollars strong,
And we but drops that bear compulsory part
In the dumb throb of a mechanic heart;
But Country is a shape of each man's mind
Sacred from definition, unconfined
By the cramped walls where daily drudgeries grind;
An inward vision, yet an outward birth
Of sweet familiar heaven and earth;
A brooding Presence that stirs motions blind
Of wings within our embryo being's shell
That wait but her completer spell
To make us eagle-natured, fit to dare
Life's nobler spaces and untarnished air.

III

You, who hold dear this self-conceived ideal,
Whose faith and works alone can make it real,
Bring all your fairest gifts to deck her shrine
Who lifts our lives away from Thine and Mine
And feeds the lamp of manhood more divine
With fragrant oils of quenchless constancy.
When all have done their utmost, surely he
Hath given the best who gives a character
Erect and constant, which nor any shock
Of loosened elements, nor the forceful sea
Of flowing or of ebbing fates, can stir

From its deep bases in the living rock
Of ancient manhood's sweet security:
And this he gave, serenely far from pride
As baseness, boon with prosperous stars allied,
Part of what nobler seed shall in our loins abide.

IV

No bond of men as common pride so strong,
In names time-filtered for the lips of song,
Still operant, with the primal Forces bound
Whose currents, on their spiritual round,
Transfuse our mortal will nor are gainsaid:
These are their arsenals, these the exhaustless
      mines
That give a constant heart in great designs;
These are the stuff whereof such dreams are made
As make heroic men: thus surely he
Still holds in place the massy blocks he laid
'Neath our new frame, enforcing soberly
The self-control that makes and keeps a people
      free.

V

I

Oh, for a drop of that Cornelian ink
Which gave Agricola dateless length of days,
To celebrate him fitly, neither swerve
To phrase unkempt, nor pass discretion's brink,
With him so statue-like in sad reserve,
So diffident to claim, so forward to deserve!

Nor need I shun due influence of his fame
Who, mortal among mortals, seemed as now
The equestrian shape with unimpassioned brow,
That paces silent on through vistas of acclaim.

II

What figure more immovably august
Than that grave strength so patient and so pure,
Calm in good fortune, when it wavered, sure,
That mind serene, impenetrably just,
Modelled on classic lines so simple they endure ?
That soul so softly radiant and so white
The track it left seems less of fire than light,
Cold but to such as love distemperature ?
And if pure light, as some deem, be the force
That drives rejoicing planets on their course,
Why for his power benign seek an impurer
        source ?
His was the true enthusiasm that burns long,
Domestically bright,
Fed from itself and shy of human sight,
The hidden force that makes a lifetime strong,
And not the short-lived fuel of a song.
Passionless, say you ? What is passion for
But to sublime our natures and control,
To front heroic toils with late return,
Or none, or such as shames the conqueror ?
That fire was fed with substance of the soul
And not with holiday stubble, that could burn,
Unpraised of men who after bonfires run,
Through seven slow years of unadvancing war,
Equal when fields were lost or fields were won,

With breath of popular applause or blame,
Nor fanned nor damped, unquenchably the same,
Too inward to be reached by flaws of idle fame.

III

Soldier and statesman, rarest unison;
High-poised example of great duties done
Simply as breathing, a world's honors worn
As life's indifferent gifts to all men born;
Dumb for himself, unless it were to God,
But for his barefoot soldiers eloquent,
Tramping the snow to coral where they trod,
Held by his awe in hollow-eyed content;
Modest, yet firm as Nature's self; unblamed
Save by the men his nobler temper shamed;
Never seduced through show of present good
By other than unsetting lights to steer
New-trimmed in Heaven, nor than his steadfast
        mood
More steadfast, far from rashness as from fear;
Rigid, but with himself first, grasping still
In swerveless poise the wave-beat helm of will;
Not honored then or now because he wooed
The popular voice, but that he still withstood;
Broad-minded, higher-souled, there is but one
Who was all this and ours, and all men's, — WASH-
        INGTON.

IV

Minds strong by fits, irregularly great,
That flash and darken like revolving lights,
Catch more the vulgar eye unschooled to wait

On the long curve of patient days and nights
Rounding a whole life to the circle fair
Of orbed fulfilment; and this balanced soul,
So simple in its grandeur, coldly bare
Of draperies theatric, standing there
In perfect symmetry of self-control,
Seems not so great at first, but greater grows
Still as we look, and by experience learn
How grand this quiet is, how nobly stern
The discipline that wrought through lifelong
      throes
That energetic passion of repose.

v

A nature too decorous and severe,
Too self-respectful in its griefs and joys,
For ardent girls and boys
Who find no genius in a mind so clear
That its grave depths seem obvious and near,
Nor a soul great that made so little noise.
They feel no force in that calm-cadenced phrase,
The habitual full-dress of his well-bred mind,
That seems to pace the minuet's courtly maze
And tell of ampler leisures, roomier length of
      days.
His firm-based brain, to self so little kind
That no tumultuary blood could blind,
Formed to control men, not amaze,
Looms not like those that borrow height of haze:
It was a world of statelier movement then
Than this we fret in, he a denizen
Of that ideal Rome that made a man for men.

VI

I

The longer on this earth we live
And weigh the various qualities of men,
Seeing how most are fugitive,
Or fitful gifts, at best, of now and then,
Wind-wavered corpse-lights, daughters of the fen,
The more we feel the high stern-featured beauty
Of plain devotedness to duty,
Steadfast and still, nor paid with mortal praise,
But finding amplest recompense
For life's ungarlanded expense
In work done squarely and unwasted days.
For this we honor him, that he could know
How sweet the service and how free
Of her, God's eldest daughter here below,
And choose in meanest raiment which was she.

II

Placid completeness, life without a fall
From faith or highest aims, truth's breachless wall,
Surely if any fame can bear the touch,
His will say " Here ! " at the last trumpet's call,
The unexpressive man whose life expressed so much.

VII

I

Never to see a nation born
Hath been given to mortal man,

Unless to those who, on that summer morn,
Gazed silent when the great Virginian
Unsheathed the sword whose fatal flash
Shot union through the incoherent clash
Of our loose atoms, crystallizing them
Around a single will's unpliant stem,
And making purpose of emotion rash.
Out of that scabbard sprang, as from its womb,
Nebulous at first but hardening to a star,
Through mutual share of sunburst and of gloom,
The common faith that made us what we are.

II

That lifted blade transformed our jangling clans,
Till then provincial, to Americans,
And made a unity of wildering plans;
Here was the doom fixed: here is marked the date
When this New World awoke to man's estate,
Burnt its last ship and ceased to look behind:
Nor thoughtless was the choice; no love or hate
Could from its poise move that deliberate mind,
Weighing between too early and too late
Those pitfalls of the man refused by Fate:
His was the impartial vision of the great
Who see not as they wish, but as they find.
He saw the dangers of defeat, nor less
The incomputable perils of success;
The sacred past thrown by, an empty rind;
The future, cloud-land, snare of prophets blind;
The waste of war, the ignominy of peace;
On either hand a sullen rear of woes,
Whose garnered lightnings none could guess,

Piling its thunder-heads and muttering " Cease ! "
Yet drew not back his hand, but gravely chose
The seeming-desperate task whence our new nation
    rose.

III

A noble choice and of immortal seed !
Nor deem that acts heroic wait on chance,
Or easy were as in a boy's romance ;
The man's whole life preludes the single deed
That shall decide if his inheritance
Be with the sifted few of matchless breed,
Our race's sap and sustenance,
Or with the unmotived herd that only sleep and
    feed.
Choice seems a thing indifferent ; thus or so,
What matters it ? The Fates with mocking face
Look on inexorable, nor seem to know
Where the lot lurks that gives life's foremost place.
Yet Duty's leaden casket holds it still,
And but two ways are offered to our will,
Toil with rare triumph, ease with safe disgrace,
The problem still for us and all of human race.
He chose, as men choose, where most danger showed,
Nor ever faltered 'neath the load
Of petty cares, that gall great hearts the most,
But kept right on the strenuous uphill road,
Strong to the end, above complaint or boast.
The popular tempest on his rock-mailed coast
Wasted its wind-borne spray,
The noisy marvel of a day ;
His soul sate still in its unstormed abode.

VIII

Virginia gave us this imperial man
Cast in the massive mould
Of those high-statured ages old
Which into grander forms our mortal metal ran;
She gave us this unblemished gentleman:
What shall we give her back but love and praise
As in the dear old unestrangèd days
Before the inevitable wrong began?
Mother of States and undiminished men,
Thou gavest us a country, giving him,
And we owe alway what we owed thee then:
The boon thou wouldst have snatched from us agen
Shines as before with no abatement dim.
A great man's memory is the only thing
With influence to outlast the present whim
And bind us as when here he knit our golden ring.
All of him that was subject to the hours
Lies in thy soil and makes it part of ours:
Across more recent graves,
Where unresentful Nature waves
Her pennons o'er the shot-ploughed sod,
Proclaiming the sweet Truce of God,
We from this consecrated plain stretch out
Our hands as free from afterthought or doubt
As here the united North
Poured her embrownèd manhood forth
In welcome of our savior and thy son.
Through battle we have better learned thy worth,
The long-breathed valor and undaunted will,

Which, like his own, the day's disaster done,
Could, safe in manhood, suffer and be still.
Both thine and ours the victory hardly won;
If ever with distempered voice or pen
We have misdeemed thee, here we take it back,
And for the dead of both don common black.
Be to us evermore as thou wast then,
As we forget thou hast not always been,
Mother of States and unpolluted men,
Virginia, fitly named from England's manly queen!

AN ODE

FOR THE FOURTH OF JULY 1876

I

1

ENTRANCED I saw a vision in the cloud
That loitered dreaming in yon sunset sky,
Full of fair shapes, half creatures of the eye,
Half chance-evoked by the wind's fantasy
In golden mist, an ever-shifting crowd:
There, 'mid unreal forms that came and went
In air-spun robes, of evanescent dye,
A woman's semblance shone preëminent;
Not armed like Pallas, not like Hera proud,
But, as on household diligence intent,
Beside her visionary wheel she bent
Like Aretë or Bertha, nor than they

v

Less queenly in her port : about her knee
Glad children clustered confident in play :
Placid her pose, the calm of energy ;
And over her broad brow in many a round
(That loosened would have gilt her garment's hem),
Succinct, as toil prescribes, the hair was wound
In lustrous coils, a natural diadem.
The cloud changed shape, obsequious to the whim
Of some transmuting influence felt in me,
And, looking now, a wolf I seemed to see
Limned in that vapor, gaunt and hunger-bold,
Threatening her charge : resolve in every limb,
Erect she flamed in mail of sun-wove gold,
Penthesilea's self for battle dight ;
One arm uplifted braced a flickering spear,
And one her adamantine shield made light ;
Her face, helm-shadowed, grew a thing to fear,
And her fierce eyes, by danger challenged, took
Her trident-sceptred mother's dauntless look.
" I know thee now, O goddess-born ! " I cried,
And turned with loftier brow and firmer stride ;
For in that spectral cloud-work I had seen
Her image, bodied forth by love and pride,
The fearless, the benign, the mother-eyed,
The fairer world's toil-consecrated queen.

II

What shape by exile dreamed elates the mind
Like hers whose hand, a fortress of the poor,
No blood in vengeance spilt, though lawful, stains?
Who never turned a suppliant from her door ?
Whose conquests are the gains of all mankind ?

To-day her thanks shall fly on every wind,
Unstinted, unrebuked, from shore to shore,
One love, one hope, and not a doubt behind !
Cannon to cannon shall repeat her praise,
Banner to banner flap it forth in flame ;
Her children shall rise up to bless her name,
And wish her harmless length of days,
The mighty mother of a mighty brood,
Blessed in all tongues and dear to every blood,
The beautiful, the strong, and, best of all, the good.

III

Seven years long was the bow
Of battle bent, and the heightening
Storm-heaps convulsed with the throe
Of their uncontainable lightning ;
Seven years long heard the sea
Crash of navies and wave-borne thunder ;
Then drifted the cloud-rack alee,
And new stars were seen, a world's wonder
Each by her sisters made bright,
All binding all to their stations,
Cluster of manifold light
Startling the old constellations :
Men looked up and grew pale :
Was it a comet or star,
Omen of blessing or bale,
Hung o'er the ocean afar ?

IV

Stormy the day of her birth :
Was she not born of the strong,

She, the last ripeness of earth,
Beautiful, prophesied long?
Stormy the days of her prime:
Hers are the pulses that beat
Higher for perils sublime,
Making them fawn at her feet.
Was she not born of the strong?
Was she not born of the wise?
Daring and counsel belong
Of right to her confident eyes:
Human and motherly they,
Careless of station or race:
Hearken! her children to-day
Shout for the joy of her face.

II

I

No praises of the past are hers,
No fanes by hallowing time caressed,
No broken arch that ministers
To Time's sad instinct in the breast:
She has not gathered from the years
Grandeur of tragedies and tears,
Nor from long leisure the unrest
That finds repose in forms of classic grace:
These may delight the coming race
Who haply shall not count it to our crime
That we who fain would sing are here before
          our time.
She also hath her monuments;

Not such as stand decrepitly resigned
To ruin-mark the path of dead events
That left no seed of better days behind,
The tourist's pensioners that show their scars
And maunder of forgotten wars ;
She builds not on the ground, but in the mind,
Her open-hearted palaces
For larger-thoughted men with heaven and earth at
      ease :
Her march the plump mow marks, the sleepless wheel,
The golden sheaf, the self-swayed commonweal ;
The happy homesteads hid in orchard trees
Whose sacrificial smokes through peaceful air
Rise lost in heaven, the household's silent prayer ;
What architect hath bettered these ?
With softened eye the westward traveller sees
A thousand miles of neighbors side by side,
Holding by toil-won titles fresh from God
The lands no serf or seigneur ever trod,
With manhood latent in the very sod,
Where the long billow of the wheat-field's tide
Flows to the sky across the prairie wide,
A sweeter vision than the castled Rhine,
Kindly with thoughts of Ruth and Bible-days benign.

II

O ancient commonwealths, that we revere
Haply because we could not know you near,
Your deeds like statues down the aisles of Time
Shine peerless in memorial calm sublime,
And Athens is a trumpet still, and Rome ;
Yet which of your achievements is not foam

Weighed with this one of hers (below you far
In fame, and born beneath a milder star),
That to Earth's orphans, far as curves the dome
Of death-deaf sky, the bounteous West means home,
With dear precedency of natural ties
That stretch from roof to roof and make men gently
      wise?
And if the nobler passions wane,
Distorted to base use, if the near goal
Of insubstantial gain
Tempt from the proper race-course of the soul
That crowns their patient breath
Whose feet, song-sandalled, are too fleet for Death,
Yet may she claim one privilege urbane,
And haply first upon the civic roll,
That none can breathe her air nor grow humane.

III

Oh, better far the briefest hour
Of Athens self-consumed, whose plastic power
Hid Beauty safe from Death in words or stone;
Of Rome, fair quarry where those eagles crowd
Whose fulgurous vans about the world had blown
Triumphant storm and seeds of polity;
Of Venice, fading o'er her shipless sea,
Last iridescence of a sunset cloud;
Than this inert prosperity,
This bovine comfort in the sense alone!
Yet art came slowly even to such as those,
Whom no past genius cheated of their own
With prudence of o'ermastering precedent;
Petal by petal spreads the perfect rose,

Secure of the divine event;
And only children rend the bud half-blown
To forestall Nature in her calm intent:
Time hath a quiver full of purposes
Which miss not of their aim, to us unknown,
And brings about the impossible with ease:
Haply for us the ideal dawn shall break
From where in legend-tinted line
The peaks of Hellas drink the morning's wine,
To tremble on our lids with mystic sign
Till the drowsed ichor in our veins awake
And set our pulse in tune with moods divine:
Long the day lingered in its sea fringed nest,
Then touched the Tuscan hills with golden lance
And paused; then on to Spain and France
The splendor flew, and Albion's misty crest:
Shall Ocean bar him from his destined West?
Or are we, then, arrived too late,
Doomed with the rest to grope disconsolate,
Foreclosed of Beauty by our modern date?

III

I

Poets, as their heads grow gray,
Look from too far behind the eyes,
Too long-experienced to be wise
In guileless youth's diviner way;
Life sings not now, but prophesies;
Time's shadows they no more behold,
But, under them, the riddle old

That mocks, bewilders, and defies:
In childhood's face the seed of shame,
In the green tree an ambushed flame,
In Phosphor a vaunt-guard of Night,
They, though against their will, divine,
And dread the care-dispelling wine
Stored from the Muse's vintage bright,
By age imbued with second-sight.
From Faith's own eyelids there peeps out,
Even as they look, the leer of doubt;
The festal wreath their fancy loads
With care that whispers and forebodes:
Nor this our triumph-day can blunt Megæra's
    goads.

II

Murmur of many voices in the air
Denounces us degenerate,
Unfaithful guardians of a noble fate,
And prompts indifference or despair:
Is this the country that we dreamed in youth,
Where wisdom and not numbers should have
    weight,
Seed-field of simpler manners, braver truth,
Where shams should cease to dominate
In household, church, and state?
Is this Atlantis? This the unpoisoned soil,
Sea-whelmed for ages and recovered late,
Where parasitic greed no more should coil
Round Freedom's stem to bend awry and blight
What grew so fair, sole plant of love and light?
Who sit where once in crowned seclusion sate

The long-proved athletes of debate
Trained from their youth, as none thinks needful
       now ?
Is this debating club where boys dispute,
And wrangle o'er their stolen fruit,
The Senate, erewhile cloister of the few,
Where Clay once flashed and Webster's cloudy
       brow
Brooded those bolts of thought that all the horizon
       knew ?

III

Oh, as this pensive moonlight blurs my pines,
Here while I sit and meditate these lines,
To gray-green dreams of what they are by day,
So would some light, not reason's sharp-edged ray,
Trance me in moonshine as before the flight
Of years had won me this unwelcome right
To see things as they are, or shall be soon,
In the frank prose of undissembling noon !

IV

Back to my breast, ungrateful sigh
Whoever fails, whoever errs,
The penalty be ours, not hers !
The present still seems vulgar, seen too nigh ;
The golden age is still the age that 's past :
I ask no drowsy opiate
To dull my vision of that only state
Founded on faith in man, and therefore sure to
       last.
For, O my country, touched by thee,

The gray hairs gather back their gold;
Thy thought sets all my pulses free;
The heart refuses to be old;
The love is all that I can see.
Not to thy natal-day belong
Time's prudent doubt or age's wrong,
But gifts of gratitude and song:
Unsummoned crowd the thankful words,
As sap in spring-time floods the tree,
Foreboding the return of birds,
For all that thou hast been to me!

IV

I

Flawless his heart and tempered to the core
Who, beckoned by the forward-leaning wave,
First left behind him the firm-footed shore,
And, urged by every nerve of sail and oar,
Steered for the Unknown which gods to mortals
        gave,
Of thought and action the mysterious door,
Bugbear of fools, a summons to the brave:
Strength found he in the unsympathizing sun,
And strange stars from beneath the horizon won,
And the dumb ocean pitilessly grave:
High-hearted surely he;
But bolder they who first off-cast
Their moorings from the habitable Past
And ventured chartless on the sea
Of storm-engendering Liberty:

For all earth's width of waters is a span,
And their convulsed existence mere repose,
Matched with the unstable heart of man,
Shoreless in wants, mist-girt in all it knows,
Open to every wind of sect or clan,
And sudden-passionate in ebbs and flows.

II

They steered by stars the elder shipmen knew,
And laid their courses where the currents draw
Of ancient wisdom channelled deep in law,
The undaunted few
Who changed the Old World for the New,
And more devoutly prized
Than all perfection theorized
The more imperfect that had roots and grew.
They founded deep and well,
Those danger-chosen chiefs of men
Who still believed in Heaven and Hell,
Nor hoped to find a spell,
In some fine flourish of a pen,
To make a better man
Than long-considering Nature will or can,
Secure against his own mistakes,
Content with what life gives or takes,
And acting still on some fore-ordered plan,
A cog of iron in an iron wheel,
Too nicely poised to think or feel,
Dumb motor in a clock-like commonweal.
They wasted not their brain in schemes
Of what man might be in some bubble-sphere,
As if he must be other than he seems

Because he was not what he should be here,
Postponing Time's slow proof to petulant dreams:
Yet herein they were great
Beyond the incredulous lawgivers of yore,
And wiser than the wisdom of the shelf,
That they conceived a deeper-rooted state,
Of hardier growth, alive from rind to core,
By making man sole sponsor of himself.

III

God of our fathers, Thou who wast,
Art, and shalt be when those eye-wise who flout
Thy secret presence shall be lost
In the great light that dazzles them to doubt,
We, sprung from loins of stalwart men
Whose strength was in their trust
That Thou wouldst make thy dwelling in their dust,
And walk with those a fellow citizen
Who build a city of the just,
We, who believe Life's bases rest
Beyond the probe of chemic test,
Still, like our fathers, feel Thee near,
Sure that, while lasts the immutable decree,
The land to Human Nature dear
Shall not be unbeloved of Thee.

HEARTSEASE AND RUE

FRIENDSHIP

AGASSIZ

Come
Dicesti *egli ebbe?* non viv' egli ancora?
Non fiere gli occhi suoi lo dolce lome?

I

I

THE electric nerve, whose instantaneous thrill
Makes next-door gossips of the antipodes,
Confutes poor Hope's last fallacy of ease, —
The distance that divided her from ill:
Earth sentient seems again as when of old
      The horny foot of Pan
Stamped, and the conscious horror ran
Beneath men's feet through all her fibres cold:
Space's blue walls are mined; we feel the throe
From underground of our night-mantled foe:
      The flame-winged feet
Of Trade's new Mercury, that dry-shod run
Through briny abysses dreàmless of the sun,
      Are mercilessly fleet,
      And at a bound annihilate
Ocean's prerogative of short reprieve;
      Surely ill news might wait,
And man be patient of delay to grieve:
      Letters have sympathies

And telltale faces that reveal,
  To senses finer than the eyes,
Their errand's purport ere we break the seal;
They wind a sorrow round with circumstance
To stay its feet, nor all unwarned displace
The veil that darkened from our sidelong glance
    The inexorable face:
  But now Fate stuns as with a mace;
The savage of the skies, that men have caught
    And some scant use of language taught,
      Tells only what he must,—
The steel-cold fact in one laconic thrust.

II

So thought I, as, with vague, mechanic eyes,
I scanned the festering news we half despise
    Yet scramble for no less,
And read of public scandal, private fraud,
Crime flaunting scot-free while the mob applaud,
Office made vile to bribe unworthiness,
    And all the unwholesome mess
The Land of Honest Abraham serves of late
    To teach the Old World how to wait,
      When suddenly,
As happens if the brain, from overweight
    Of blood, infect the eye,
Three tiny words grew lurid as I read,
And reeled commingling: *Agassiz is dead.*
As when, beneath the street's familiar jar,
An earthquake's alien omen rumbles far,
Men listen and forebode, I hung my head,
    And strove the present to recall,
As if the blow that stunned were yet to fall.

III

 Uprooted is our mountain oak,
That promised long security of shade
And brooding-place for many a wingëd thought;
 Not by Time's softly-cadenced stroke
With pauses of relenting pity stayed,
But ere a root seemed sapt, a bough decayed,
From sudden ambush by the whirlwind caught
And in his broad maturity betrayed!

IV

Well might I, as of old, appeal to you,
 O mountains, woods, and streams,
To help us mourn him, for ye loved him too;
 But simpler moods befit our modern themes,
And no less perfect birth of nature can,
Though they yearn tow'rd him, sympathize with
  man,
Save as dumb fellow prisoners through a wall;
 Answer ye rather to my call,
Strong poets of a more unconscious day,
When Nature spake nor sought nice reasons why,
Too much for softer arts forgotten since
That teach our forthright tongue to lisp and mince,
And drown in music the heart's bitter cry!
Lead me some steps in your directer way,
Teach me those words that strike a solid root
  Within the ears of men;
Ye chiefly, virile both to think and feel,
Deep-chested Chapman and firm-footed Ben,
For he was masculine from head to heel.
Nay, let himself stand undiminished by
 v

With those clear parts of him that will not die.
Himself from out the recent dark I claim
To hear, and, if I flatter him, to blame;
To show himself, as still I seem to see,
A mortal, built upon the antique plan,
Brimful of lusty blood as ever ran,
And taking life as simply as a tree!
To claim my foiled good-bye let him appear,
Large-limbed and human as I saw him near,
Loosed from the stiffening uniform of fame:
And let me treat him largely: I should fear
(If with too prying lens I chanced to err,
Mistaking catalogue for character),
His wise forefinger raised in smiling blame.
Nor would I scant him with judicial breath
And turn mere critic in an epitaph;
I choose the wheat, incurious of the chaff
That swells fame living, chokes it after death,
And would but memorize the shining half
Of his large nature that was turned to me:
Fain had I joined with those that honored him
With eyes that darkened because his were dim,
And now been silent: but it might not be.

II

I

In some the genius is a thing apart,
       A pillared hermit of the brain,
Hoarding with incommunicable art
              Its intellectual gain;

Man's web of circumstance and fate
    They from their perch of self observe,
Indifferent as the figures on a slate
    Are to the planet's sun-swung curve
    Whose bright returns they calculate;
    Their nice adjustment, part to part,
Were shaken from its serviceable mood
By unpremeditated stirs of heart
    Or jar of human neighborhood :
Some find their natural selves, and only then,
In furloughs of divine escape from men,
And when, by that brief ecstasy left bare,
    Driven by some instinct of desire,
They wander worldward, 't is to blink and stare,
Like wild things of the wood about a fire,
Dazed by the social glow they cannot share;
    His nature brooked no lonely lair,
But basked and bourgeoned in copartnery,
Companionship, and open-windowed glee :
    He knew, for he had tried,
    Those speculative heights that lure
The unpractised foot, impatient of a guide,
    Tow'rd ether too attenuately pure
For sweet unconscious breath, though dear to pride,
    But better loved the foothold sure
Of paths that wind by old abodes of men
Who hope at last the churchyard's peace secure,
And follow time-worn rules, that them suffice,
Learned from their sires, traditionally wise,
Careful of honest custom's how and when;
His mind, too brave to look on Truth askance,
No more those habitudes of faith could share,

But, tinged with sweetness of the old Swiss manse,
Lingered around them still and fain would spare.
Patient to spy a sullen egg for weeks,
The enigma of creation to surprise,
His truer instinct sought the life that speaks
Without a mystery from kindly eyes;
In no self-spun cocoon of prudence wound,
He by the touch of men was best inspired,
And caught his native greatness at rebound
From generosities itself had fired;
Then how the heat through every fibre ran,
Felt in the gathering presence of the man,
While the apt word and gesture came unbid!
Virtues and faults it to one metal wrought,
        Fined all his blood to thought,
And ran the molten man in all he said or did.
All Tully's rules and all Quintilian's too
He by the light of listening faces knew,
And his rapt audience all unconscious lent
Their own roused force to make him eloquent;
Persuasion fondled in his look and tone;
Our speech (with strangers prudish) he could bring
To find new charm in accents not her own;
Her coy constraints and icy hindrances
Melted upon his lips to natural ease,
As a brook's fetters swell the dance of spring.
Nor yet all sweetness: not in vain he wore,
Nor in the sheath of ceremony, controlled
By velvet courtesy or caution cold,
That sword of honest anger prized of old,
        But, with two-handed wrath,
If baseness or pretension crossed his path,
        Struck once nor needed to strike more.

II

His magic was not far to seek, —
He was so human ! Whether strong or weak,
Far from his kind he neither sank nor soared,
But sate an equal guest at every board :
No beggar ever felt him condescend,
No prince presume ; for still himself he bare
At manhood's simple level, and where'er
He met a stranger, there he left a friend.
How large an aspect ! nobly unsevere,
With freshness round him of Olympian cheer,
Like visits of those earthly gods he came ;
His look, wherever its good fortune fell,
Doubled the feast without a miracle,
And on the hearthstone danced a happier flame ;
Philemon's crabbed vintage grew benign ;
Amphitryon's gold-juice humanized to wine.

III

I

The garrulous memories
Gather again from all their far-flown nooks,
Singly at first, and then by twos and threes,
Then in a throng innumerable, as the rooks
  Thicken their twilight files
Tow'rd Tintern's gray repose of roofless aisles :
Once more I see him at the table's head
When Saturday her monthly banquet spread
  To scholars, poets, wits,

All choice, some famous, loving things, not names,
And so without a twinge at others' fames;
Such company as wisest moods befits,
Yet with no pedant blindness to the worth
 Of undeliberate mirth,
Natures benignly mixed of air and earth,
Now with the stars and now with equal zest
Tracing the eccentric orbit of a jest.

II

I see in vision the warm-lighted hall,
The living and the dead I see again,
And but my chair is empty; 'mid them all
'T is I that seem the dead: they all remain
Immortal, changeless creatures of the brain:
Well-nigh I doubt which world is real most,
Of sense or spirit, to the truly sane;
In this abstraction it were light to deem
Myself the figment of some stronger dream;
They are the real things, and I the ghost
That glide unhindered through the solid door,
Vainly for recognition seek from chair to chair,
And strive to speak and am but futile air,
As truly most of us are little more.

III

Him most I see whom we most dearly miss,
 The latest parted thence,
His features poised in genial armistice
And armed neutrality of self-defence
Beneath the forehead's walled preëminence,
While Tyro, plucking facts with careless reach,

Settles off-hand our human how and whence;
The long-trained veteran scarcely wincing hears
The infallible strategy of volunteers
Making through Nature's walls its easy breach,
And seems to learn where he alone could teach.
Ample and ruddy, the board's end he fills
As he our fireside were, our light and heat,
Centre where minds diverse and various skills
Find their warm nook and stretch unhampered
        feet;
I see the firm benignity of face,
Wide-smiling champaign, without tameness sweet,
The mass Teutonic toned to Gallic grace,
The eyes whose sunshine runs before the lips
While Holmes's rockets curve their long ellipse,
        And burst in seeds of fire that burst again
                To drop in scintillating rain.

                        IV

There too the face half-rustic, half-divine,
Self-poised, sagacious, freaked with humor fine,
Of him who taught us not to mow and mope
About our fancied selves, but seek our scope
In Nature's world and Man's, nor fade to hollow
        trope,
Content with our New World and timely bold
To challenge the o'ermastery of the Old;
Listening with eyes averse I see him sit
Pricked with the cider of the Judge's wit
(Ripe-hearted homebrew, fresh and fresh again),
While the wise nose's firm-built aquiline
        Curves sharper to restrain

The merriment whose most unruly moods
Pass not the dumb laugh learned in listening woods
    Of silence-shedding pine.
Hard-by is he whose art's consoling spell
Hath given both worlds a whiff of asphodel,
His look still vernal 'mid the wintry ring
Of petals that remember, not foretell,
The paler primrose of a second spring.

V

And more there are : but other forms arise
And seen as clear, albeit with dimmer eyes :
First he from sympathy still held apart
By shrinking over-eagerness of heart,
Cloud charged with searching fire, whose shadow's
    sweep
Heightened mean things with sense of brooding ill,
And steeped in doom familiar field and hill, —
New England's poet, soul reserved and deep,
November nature with a name of May,
Whom high o'er Concord plains we laid to sleep,
While the orchards mocked us in their white array
And building robins wondered at our tears,
Snatched in his prime, the shape august
That should have stood unbent 'neath fourscore years,
The noble head, the eyes of furtive trust,
    All gone to speechless dust.
    And he our passing guest,
Shy nature, too, and stung with life's unrest,
Whom we too briefly had but could not hold,
Who brought ripe Oxford's culture to our board,
    The Past's incalculable hoard,

Mellowed by scutcheoned panes in cloisters old,
Seclusions ivy-hushed, and pavements sweet
With immemorial lisp of musing feet;
Young head time-tonsured smoother than a friar's,
Boy face, but grave with answerless desires,
Poet in all that poets have of best,
But foiled with riddles dark and cloudy aims,
 Who now hath found sure rest,
Not by still Isis or historic Thames,
Nor by the Charles he tried to love with me,
But, not misplaced, by Arno's hallowed brim,
Nor scorned by Santa Croce's neighboring fames,
 Haply not mindless, wheresoe'er he be,
Of violets that to-day I scattered over him;
 He, too, is there,
 After the good centurion fitly named,
 Whom learning dulled not, nor convention tamed,
 Shaking with burly mirth his hyacinthine hair,
 Our hearty Grecian of Homeric ways,
Still found the surer friend where least he hoped the
 praise.

VI

 Yea truly, as the sallowing years
Fall from us faster, like frost-loosened leaves
Pushed by the misty touch of shortening days,
 And that unwakened winter nears,
'T is the void chair our surest guest receives,
'T is lips long cold that give the warmest kiss,
'T is the lost voice comes oftenest to our ears;
We count our rosary by the beads we miss:
 To me, at least, it seemeth so,

An exile in the land once found divine,
      While my starved fire burns low,
And homeless winds at the loose casement whine
Shrill ditties of the snow-roofed Apennine.

IV

1

Now forth into the darkness all are gone,
But memory, still unsated, follows on,
Retracing step by step our homeward walk,
With many a laugh among our serious talk,
Across the bridge where, on the dimpling tide,
The long red streamers from the windows glide,
      Or the dim western moon
Rocks her skiff's image on the broad lagoon,
And Boston shows a soft Venetian side
In that Arcadian light when roof and tree,
Hard prose by daylight, dream in Italy;
Or haply in the sky's cold chambers wide
Shivered the winter stars, while all below,
As if an end were come of human ill,
The world was wrapt in innocence of snow
And the cast-iron bay was blind and still;
These were our poetry; in him perhaps
Science had barred the gate that lets in dream,
And he would rather count the perch and bream
Than with the current's idle fancy lapse;
And yet he had the poet's open eye
That takes a frank delight in all it sees,
Nor was earth voiceless, nor the mystic sky,

To him the lifelong friend of fields and trees :
Then came the prose of the suburban street,
Its silence deepened by our echoing feet,
And converse such as rambling hazard finds ;
Then he who many cities knew and many minds,
And men once world-noised, now mere Ossian forms
Of misty memory, bade them live anew
As when they shared earth's manifold delight,
In shape, in gait, in voice, in gesture true,
And, with an accent heightening as he warms,
Would stop forgetful of the shortening night,
Drop my confining arm, and pour profuse
Much worldly wisdom kept for others' use,
Not for his own, for he was rash and free,
His purse or knowledge all men's, like the sea.
Still can I hear his voice's shrilling might
(With pauses broken, while the fitful spark
He blew more hotly rounded on the dark
To hint his features with a Rembrandt light)
Call Oken back, or Humboldt, or Lamarck,
Or Cuvier's taller shade, and many more
Whom he had seen, or knew from others' sight,
And make them men to me as ne'er before :
Not seldom, as the undeadened fibre stirred
Of noble friendships knit beyond the sea,
German or French thrust by the lagging word,
For a good leash of mother tongues had he.
At last, arrived at where our paths divide,
" Good-night ! " and, ere the distance grew too
          wide,
" Good-night ! " again ; and now with cheated ear
I half hear his who mine shall never hear.

II

Sometimes it seemed as if New England air
For his large lungs too parsimonious were,
As if those empty rooms of dogma drear
Where the ghost shivers of a faith austere
     Counting the horns o'er of the Beast,
Still scaring those whose faith in it is least,
As if those snaps o' th' moral atmosphere
That sharpen all the needles of the East,
     Had been to him like death,
Accustomed to draw Europe's freer breath
     In a more stable element;
Nay, even our landscape, half the year morose,
Our practical horizon grimly pent,
Our air, sincere of ceremonious haze,
Forcing hard outlines mercilessly close,
Our social monotone of level days,
     Might make our best seem banishment;
        But it was nothing so;
     Haply his instinct might divine,
Beneath our drift of puritanic snow,
     The marvel sensitive and fine
Of sanguinaria over-rash to blow
And trust its shyness to an air malign;
Well might he prize truth's warranty and pledge
In the grim outcrop of our granite edge,
Or Hebrew fervor flashing forth at need
In the gaunt sons of Calvin's iron breed,
As prompt to give as skilled to win and keep;
But though such intuitions might not cheer,
Yet life was good to him, and, there or here,

With that sufficing joy, the day was never cheap;
Thereto his mind was its own ample sphere,
And, like those buildings great that through the
        year
Carry one temperature, his nature large
Made its own climate, nor could any marge
Traced by convention stay him from his bent:
He had a habitude of mountain air;
He brought wide outlook where he went,
        And could on sunny uplands dwell
Of prospect sweeter than the pastures fair
        High-hung of viny Neufchâtel;
                Nor, surely, did he miss
                Some pale, imaginary bliss
Of earlier sights whose inner landscape still was
        Swiss.

V

I

I cannot think he wished so soon to die
With all his senses full of eager heat,
And rosy years that stood expectant by
To buckle the winged sandals on their feet,
He that was friends with Earth, and all her sweet
Took with both hands unsparingly:
Truly this life is precious to the root,
And good the feel of grass beneath the foot;
To lie in buttercups and clover-bloom,
        Tenants in common with the bees,
And watch the white clouds drift through gulfs
        of trees,

Is better than long waiting in the tomb;
    Only once more to feel the coming spring
As the birds feel it, when it bids them sing,
Only once more to see the moon
Through leaf-fringed abbey-arches of the elms
    Curve her mild sickle in the West
Sweet with the breath of hay-cocks, were a boon
Worth any promise of soothsayer realms
Or casual hope of being elsewhere blest;
    To take December by the beard
And crush the creaking snow with springy foot,
While overhead the North's dumb streamers
    shoot,
Till Winter fawn upon the cheek endeared,
    Then the long evening-ends
    Lingered by cosy chimney-nooks,
With high companionship of books
    Or slippered talk of friends
    And sweet habitual looks,
Is better than to stop the ears with dust:
Too soon the spectre comes to say, " Thou must!"

II

When toil-crooked hands are crost upon the breast,
    They comfort us with sense of rest;
They must be glad to lie forever still;
    Their work is ended with their day;
Another fills their room; 't is the World's ancient
    way,
    Whether for good or ill;
But the deft spinners of the brain,
Who love each added day and find it gain,

Them overtakes the doom
To snap the half-grown flower upon the loom
(Trophy that was to be of lifelong pain),
The thread no other skill can ever knit again.
    'T was so with him, for he was glad to live,
      'T was doubly so, for he left work begun;
Could not this eagerness of Fate forgive
      Till all the allotted flax were spun?
It matters not; for, go at night or noon,
A friend, whene'er he dies, has died too soon,
And, once we hear the hopeless *He is dead*,
So far as flesh hath knowledge, all is said.

VI

I

I seem to see the black procession go:
That crawling prose of death too well I know,
The vulgar paraphrase of glorious woe;
I see it wind through that unsightly grove,
Once beautiful, but long defaced
With granite permanence of cockney taste
And all those grim disfigurements we love:
There, then, we leave him: Him? such costly
        waste
Nature rebels at: and it is not true
Of those most precious parts of him we knew:
Could we be conscious but as dreamers be,
'T were sweet to leave this shifting life of tents
Sunk in the changeless calm of Deity;
Nay, to be mingled with the elements,

The fellow servant of creative powers,
Partaker in the solemn year's events,
To share the work of busy-fingered hours,
To be night's silent almoner of dew,
To rise again in plants and breathe and grow,
To stream as tides the ocean caverns through,
Or with the rapture of great winds to blow
About earth's shaken coignes, were not a fate
    To leave us all-disconsolate;
Even endless slumber in the sweetening sod
     Of charitable earth
That takes out all our mortal stains,
And makes us cleanlier neighbors of the clod,
    Methinks were better worth
Than the poor fruit of most men's wakeful pains,
    The heart's insatiable ache:
    But such was not his faith,
Nor mine: it may be he had trod
Outside the plain old path of *God thus spake,*
    But God to him was very God,
    And not a visionary wraith
Skulking in murky corners of the mind,
    And he was sure to be
Somehow, somewhere, imperishable as He,
Not with His essence mystically combined,
As some high spirits long, but whole and free,
    A perfected and conscious Agassiz.
And such I figure him: the wise of old
Welcome and own him of their peaceful fold,
    Not truly with the guild enrolled
    Of him who seeking inward guessed
    Diviner riddles than the rest,

And groping in the darks of thought
Touched the Great Hand and knew it not;
Rather he shares the daily light,
From reason's charier fountains won,
Of his great chief, the slow-paced Stagyrite,
And Cuvier clasps once more his long-lost son.

II

The shape erect is prone : forever stilled
The winning tongue; the forehead's high-piled
    heap,
A cairn which every science helped to build,
Unvalued will its golden secrets keep:
He knows at last if Life or Death be best :
Wherever he be flown, whatever vest
The being hath put on which lately here
So many-friended was, so full of cheer
To make men feel the Seeker's noble zest,
We have not lost him all; he is not gone
To the dumb herd of them that wholly die ;
The beauty of his better self lives on
In minds he touched with fire, in many an eye
He trained to Truth's exact severity;
He was a Teacher : why be grieved for him
Whose living word still stimulates the air ?
In endless file shall loving scholars come
The glow of his transmitted touch to share,
And trace his features with an eye less dim
Than ours whose sense familiar wont makes
    numb.

FLORENCE, ITALY, February, 1874.

    V

TO HOLMES

ON HIS SEVENTY-FIFTH BIRTHDAY

DEAR WENDELL, why need count the years
  Since first your genius made me thrill,
If what moved then to smiles or tears,
  Or both contending, move me still?

What has the Calendar to do
  With poets? What Time's fruitless tooth
With gay immortals such as you
  Whose years but emphasize your youth?

One air gave both their lease of breath;
  The same paths lured our boyish feet;
One earth will hold us safe in death
  With dust of saints and scholars sweet.

Our legends from one source were drawn,
  I scarce distinguish yours from mine,
And *don't* we make the Gentiles yawn
  With "You remembers?" o'er our wine!

If I, with too senescent air,
  Invade your elder memory's pale,
You snub me with a pitying " Where
  Were you in the September Gale?"

Both stared entranced at Lafayette,
　　Saw Jackson dubbed with LL. D.
What Cambridge saw not strikes us yet
　　As scarcely worth one's while to see.

Ten years my senior, when my name
　　In Harvard's entrance-book was writ,
Her halls still echoed with the fame
　　Of you, her poet and her wit.

'T is fifty years from then to now :
　　But your Last Leaf renews its green,
Though, for the laurels on your brow
　　(So thick they crowd), 't is hardly seen.

The oriole's fledglings fifty times
　　Have flown from our familiar elms ;
As many poets with their rhymes
　　Oblivion's darkling dust o'erwhelms.

The birds are hushed, the poets gone
　　Where no harsh critic's lash can reach,
And still your wingèd brood sing on
　　To all who love our English speech.

Nay, let the foolish records be
　　That make believe you 're seventy-five :
You 're the old Wendell still to me, —
　　And that 's the youngest man alive.

The gray-blue eyes, I see them still,
　　The gallant front with brown o'erhung,
The shape alert, the wit at will,
　　The phrase that stuck, but never stung.

You keep your youth as yon Scotch firs,
  Whose gaunt line my horizon hems,
Though twilight all the lowland blurs,
  Hold sunset in their ruddy stems.

You with the elders ? Yes, 't is true,
  But in no sadly literal sense,
With elders and coevals too,
  Whose verb admits no preterite tense.

Master alike in speech and song
  Of fame's great antiseptic — Style,
You with the classic few belong
  Who tempered wisdom with a smile.

Outlive us all ! Who else like you
  Could sift the seedcorn from our chaff,
And make us with the pen we knew
  Deathless at least in epitaph ?

WOLLASTON, August 29, 1884.

IN A COPY OF OMAR KHAYYÁM

THESE pearls of thought in Persian gulfs were
        bred,
Each softly lucent as a rounded moon ;
The diver Omar plucked them from their bed,
FitzGerald strung them on an English thread.

Fit rosary for a queen, in shape and hue,
When Contemplation tells her pensive beads
Of mortal thoughts, forever old and new.
Fit for a queen? Why, surely then for you!

The moral? Where Doubt's eddies toss and twirl
Faith's slender shallop till her footing reel,
Plunge: if you find not peace beneath the whirl,
Groping, you may like Omar grasp a pearl.

ON RECEIVING A COPY OF MR. AUSTIN DOBSON'S "OLD WORLD IDYLLS"

I

At length arrived, your book I take
To read in for the author's sake;
Too gray for new sensations grown,
Can charm to Art or Nature known
This torpor from my senses shake?

Hush! my parched ears what runnels slake?
Is a thrush gurgling from the brake?
Has Spring, on all the breezes blown,
At length arrived?

Long may you live such songs to make,
And I to listen while you wake,
With skill of late disused, each tone
Of the *Lesboum barbiton*,
At mastery, through long finger-ache,
At length arrived.

II

As I read on, what changes steal
O'er me and through, from head to heel?
A rapier thrusts coat-skirt aside,
My rough Tweeds bloom to silken pride, —
Who was it laughed? Your hand, Dick Steele!

Down vistas long of clipt *charmille*
Watteau as Pierrot leads the reel;
Tabor and pipe the dancers guide
As I read on.

While in and out the verses wheel
The wind-caught robes trim feet reveal,
Lithe ankles that to music glide,
But chastely and by chance descried;
Art? Nature? Which do I most feel
As I read on?

TO C. F. BRADFORD

ON THE GIFT OF A MEERSCHAUM PIPE

THE pipe came safe, and welcome too,
As anything must be from you;
A meerschaum pure, 't would float as light
As she the girls call Amphitrite.

Mixture divine of foam and clay,
From both it stole the best away:
Its foam is such as crowns the glow
Of beakers brimmed by Veuve Clicquot;
Its clay is but congested lymph
Jove chose to make some choicer nymph:
And here combined, — why, this must be
The birth of some enchanted sea,
Shaped to immortal form, the type
And very Venus of a pipe.

When high I heap it with the weed
From Lethe wharf, whose potent seed
Nicotia, big from Bacchus, bore
And cast upon Virginia's shore,
I'll think, — So fill the fairer bowl
And wise alembic of thy soul,
With herbs far-sought that shall distil,
Not fumes to slacken thought and will,
But bracing essences that nerve
To wait, to dare, to strive, to serve.

When curls the smoke in eddies soft,
And hangs a shifting dream aloft,
That gives and takes, though chance-designed,
The impress of the dreamer's mind,
I'll think, — So let the vapors bred
By Passion, in the heart or head,
Pass off and upward into space,
Waving farewells of tenderest grace,
Remembered in some happier time,
To blend their beauty with my rhyme.

While slowly o'er its candid bowl
The color deepens (as the soul
That burns in mortals leaves its trace
Of bale or beauty on the face),
I 'll think, — So let the essence rare
Of years consuming make me fair;
So, 'gainst the ills of life profuse,
Steep me in some narcotic juice;
And if my soul must part with all
That whiteness which we greenness call,
Smooth back, O Fortune, half thy frown,
And make me beautifully brown!

Dream-forger, I refill thy cup
With reverie's wasteful pittance up,
And while the fire burns slow away,
Hiding itself in ashes gray,
I 'll think, — As inward Youth retreats,
Compelled to spare his wasting heats,
When Life's Ash-Wednesday comes about,
And my head 's gray with fires burnt out,
While stays one spark to light the eye,
With the last flash of memory,
'T will leap to welcome C. F. B.,
Who sent my favorite pipe to me.

BANKSIDE

(HOME OF EDMUND QUINCY)

DEDHAM MAY 21 1877

I

I CHRISTENED you in happier days, before
These gray forebodings on my brow were seen;
You are still lovely in your new-leaved green;
The brimming river soothes his grassy shore;
The bridge is there; the rock with lichens hoar;
And the same shadows on the water lean,
Outlasting us. How many graves between
That day and this! How many shadows more
Darken my heart, their substance from these eyes
Hidden forever! So our world is made
Of life and death commingled; and the sighs
Outweigh the smiles, in equal balance laid:
What compensation? None, save that the All-wise
So schools us to love things that cannot fade.

II

Thank God, he saw you last in pomp of May,
Ere any leaf had felt the year's regret;
Your latest image in his memory set
Was fair as when your landscape's peaceful sway
Charmed dearer eyes with his to make delay
On Hope's long prospect, — as if They forget

The happy, They, the unspeakable Three, whose
    debt,
Like the hawk's shadow, blots our brightest day:
Better it is that ye should look so fair,
Slopes that he loved, and ever-murmuring pines
That make a music out of silent air,
And bloom-heaped orchard-trees in prosperous lines;
In you the heart some sweeter hints divines,
And wiser, than in winter's dull despair.

III

Old Friend, farewell! Your kindly door again
I enter, but the master's hand in mine
No more clasps welcome, and the temperate wine,
That cheered our long nights, other lips must stain:
All is unchanged, but I expect in vain
The face alert, the manners free and fine,
The seventy years borne lightly as the pine
Wears its first down of snow in green disdain:
Much did he, and much well; yet most of all
I prized his skill in leisure and the ease
Of a life flowing full without a plan;
For most are idly busy; him I call
Thrice fortunate who knew himself to please,
Learned in those arts that make a gentleman.

IV

Nor deem he lived unto himself alone;
His was the public spirit of his sire,
And in those eyes, soft with domestic fire,
A quenchless light of fiercer temper shone
What time about the world our shame was blown

On every wind ; his soul would not conspire
With selfish men to soothe the mob's desire,
Veiling with garlands Moloch's bloody stone ;
The high-bred instincts of a better day
Ruled in his blood, when to be citizen
Rang Roman yet, and a Free People's sway
Was not the exchequer of impoverished men,
Nor statesmanship with loaded votes to play,
Nor public office a tramps' boosing-ken.

JOSEPH WINLOCK

DIED JUNE 11 1875

SHY soul and stalwart, man of patient will
Through years one hair's-breadth on our Dark to
        gain,
Who, from the stars he studied not in vain,
Had learned their secret to be strong and still,
Careless of fames that earth's tin trumpets fill ;
Born under Leo, broad of build and brain,
While others slept, he watched in that hushed fane
Of Science, only witness of his skill :
Sudden as falls a shooting-star he fell,
But inextinguishable his luminous trace
In mind and heart of all that knew him well.
Happy man's doom ! To him the Fates were known
Of orbs dim hovering on the skirts of space,
Unprescient, through God's mercy, of his own !

SONNET

TO FANNY ALEXANDER

UNCONSCIOUS as the sunshine, simply sweet
And generous as that, thou dost not close
Thyself in art, as life were but a rose
To rumple bee-like with luxurious feet;
Thy higher mind therein finds sure retreat,
But not from care of common hopes and woes;
Thee the dark chamber, thee the unfriended, knows,
Although no babbling crowds thy praise repeat:
Consummate artist, who life's landscape bleak
Hast brimmed with sun to many a clouded eye,
Touched to a brighter hue the beggar's cheek,
Hung over orphaned lives a gracious sky,
And traced for eyes, that else would vainly seek,
Fair pictures of an angel drawing nigh!
　　FLORENCE, 1873.

JEFFRIES WYMAN

DIED SEPTEMBER 4 1874

THE wisest man could ask no more of Fate
Than to be simple, modest, manly, true,
Safe from the Many, honored by the Few;
To count as naught in World, or Church, or State,

But inwardly in secret to be great;
To feel mysterious Nature ever new;
To touch, if not to grasp, her endless clue,
And learn by each discovery how to wait.
He widened knowledge and escaped the praise;
He wisely taught, because more wise to learn;
He toiled for Science, not to draw men's gaze,
But for her lore of self-denial stern.
That such a man could spring from our decays
Fans the soul's nobler faith until it burn.

TO A FRIEND

WHO GAVE ME A GROUP OF WEEDS AND GRASSES, AFTER A DRAWING OF DÜRER

TRUE as the sun's own work, but more refined,
It tells of love behind the artist's eye,
Of sweet companionships with earth and sky,
And summers stored, the sunshine of the mind.
What peace! Sure, ere you breathe, the fickle wind
Will break its truce and bend that grass-plume high,
Scarcely yet quiet from the gilded fly
That flits a more luxurious perch to find.
Thanks for a pleasure that can never pall,
A serene moment, deftly caught and kept
To make immortal summer on my wall.
Had he who drew such gladness ever wept?
Ask rather could he else have seen at all,
Or grown in Nature's mysteries an adept?

WITH AN ARMCHAIR

I

ABOUT the oak that framed this chair, of old
The seasons danced their round; delighted wings
Brought music to its boughs; shy woodland things
Shared its broad roof, 'neath whose green glooms
     grown bold,
Lovers, more shy than they, their secret told;
The resurrection of a thousand springs
Swelled in its veins, and dim imaginings
Teased them, perchance, of life more manifold.
Such shall it know when its proud arms enclose
My Lady Goshawk, musing here at rest,
Careless of him who into exile goes,
Yet, while his gift by those fair limbs is prest,
Through some fine sympathy of nature knows
That, seas between us, she is still his guest.

II

Yet sometimes, let me dream, the conscious wood
A momentary vision may renew
Of him who counts it treasure that he knew,
Though but in passing, such a priceless good,
And, like an elder brother, felt his mood
Uplifted by the spell that kept her true,
Amid her lightsome compeers, to the few
That wear the crown of serious womanhood:
Were he so happy, think of him as one

Who in the Louvre or Pitti feels his soul
Rapt by some dead face which, till then unseen,
Moves like a memory, and, till life outrun,
Is vexed with vague misgiving, past control,
Of nameless loss and thwarted might-have-been.

E. G. DE R.

WHY should I seek her spell to decompose
Or to its source each rill of influence trace
That feeds the brimming river of her grace?
The petals numbered but degrade to prose
Summer's triumphant poem of the rose:
Enough for me to watch the wavering chase,
Like wind o'er grass, of moods across her face,
Fairest in motion, fairer in repose.
Steeped in her sunshine, let me, while I may,
Partake the bounty: ample 't is for me
That her mirth cheats my temples of their gray,
Her charm makes years long spent seem yet to be.
Wit, goodness, grace, swift flash from grave to gay,
All these are good, but better far is she.

BON VOYAGE

SHIP, blest to bear such freight across the blue,
May stormless stars control thy horoscope;
In keel and hull, in every spar and rope,
Be night and day to thy dear office true!

Ocean, men's path and their divider too,
No fairer shrine of memory and hope
To the underworld adown thy westering slope
E'er vanished, or whom such regrets pursue :
Smooth all thy surges as when Jove to Crete
Swam with less costly burthen, and prepare
A pathway meet for her home-coming soon
With golden undulations such as greet
The printless summer-sandals of the moon
And tempt the Nautilus his cruise to dare !

TO WHITTIER

ON HIS SEVENTY-FIFTH BIRTHDAY

New England's poet, rich in love as years,
Her hills and valleys praise thee, her swift brooks
Dance in thy verse; to her grave sylvan nooks
Thy steps allure us, which the wood-thrush hears
As maids their lovers', and no treason fears;
Through thee her Merrimacs and Agiochooks
And many a name uncouth win gracious looks,
Sweetly familiar to both Englands' ears:
Peaceful by birthright as a virgin lake,
The lily's anchorage, which no eyes behold
Save those of stars, yet for thy brother's sake
That lay in bonds, thou blewst a blast as bold
As that wherewith the heart of Roland brake,
Far heard across the New World and the Old.

ON AN AUTUMN SKETCH OF H. G. WILD

Thanks to the artist, ever on my wall
The sunset stays : that hill in glory rolled,
Those trees and clouds in crimson and in gold,
Burn on, nor cool when evening's shadows fall.
Not round *these* splendors Midnight wraps her pall ;
These leaves the flush of Autumn's vintage hold
In Winter's spite, nor can the Northwind bold
Deface my chapel's western window small :
On one, ah me ! October struck his frost,
But not repaid him with those Tyrian hues ;
His naked boughs but tell him what is lost,
And parting comforts of the sun refuse :
His heaven is bare, — ah, were its hollow crost
Even with a cloud whose light were yet to lose !

    April, 1854.

TO MISS D. T.

ON HER GIVING ME A DRAWING OF LITTLE STREET ARABS

As, cleansed of Tiber's and Oblivion's slime,
Glow Farnesina's vaults with shapes again
That dreamed some exiled artist from his pain
Back to his Athens and the Muse's clime,
So these world-orphaned waifs of Want and Crime,

v

Purged by Art's absolution from the stain
Of the polluting city-flood, regain
Ideal grace secure from taint of time.
An Attic frieze you gave, a pictured song;
For as with words the poet paints, for you
The happy pencil at its labor sings,
Stealing his privilege, nor does him wrong,
Beneath the false discovering the true,
And Beauty's best in unregarded things.

WITH A COPY OF AUCASSIN AND NICOLETE

LEAVES fit to have been poor Juliet's cradle-rhyme,
With gladness of a heart long quenched in mould
They vibrate still, a nest not yet grown cold
From its fledged burthen. The numb hand of Time
Vainly his glass turns; here is endless prime;
Here lips their roses keep and locks their gold;
Here Love in pristine innocency bold
Speaks what our grosser conscience makes a crime.
Because it tells the dream that all have known
Once in their lives, and to life's end the few;
Because its seeds o'er Memory's desert blown
Spring up in heartsease such as Eden knew;
Because it hath a beauty all its own,
Dear Friend, I plucked this herb of grace for you.

ON PLANTING A TREE AT INVERARAY

WHO does his duty is a question
Too complex to be solved by me,
But he, I venture the suggestion,
Does part of his that plants a tree.

For after he is dead and buried,
And epitaphed, and well forgot,
Nay, even his shade by Charon ferried
To — let us not inquire to what,

His deed, its author long outliving,
By Nature's mother-care increased,
Shall stand, his verdant almoner, giving
A kindly dole to man and beast.

The wayfarer, at noon reposing,
Shall bless its shadow on the grass,
Or sheep beneath it huddle, dozing,
Until the thundergust o'erpass.

The owl, belated in his plundering,
Shall here await the friendly night,
Blinking whene'er he wakes, and wondering
What fool it was invented light.

Hither the busy birds shall flutter,
With the light timber for their nests,
And, pausing from their labor, utter
The morning sunshine in their breasts.

What though his memory shall have vanished,
Since the good deed he did survives ?
It is not wholly to be banished
Thus to be part of many lives.

Grow, then, my foster-child, and strengthen,
Bough over bough, a murmurous pile,
And, as your stately stem shall lengthen,
So may the statelier of Argyll !

1880.

AN EPISTLE TO GEORGE WILLIAM CURTIS

" De prodome,
Des qu'il s'a torne a grant bonte
Ja n'iert tot dit ne tot conte,
Que leingue ne puet pas retraire
Tant d'enor com prodom set faire."

CRESTIEN DE TROIES,
Li Romans dou Chevalier au Lyon, 784–788.

1874

CURTIS, whose Wit, with Fancy arm in arm,
Masks half its muscle in its skill to charm,
And who so gently can the Wrong expose
As sometimes to make converts, never foes,
Or only such as good men must expect,
Knaves sore with conscience of their own defect,

I come with mild remonstrance. Ere I start,
A kindlier errand interrupts my heart,
And I must utter, though it vex your ears,
The love, the honor, felt so many years.
Curtis, skilled equally with voice and pen
To stir the hearts or mould the minds of men, —
That voice whose music, for I 've heard you sing
Sweet as Casella, can with passion ring,
That pen whose rapid ease ne'er trips with haste,
Nor scrapes nor sputters, pointed with good taste,
First Steele's, then Goldsmith's, next it came to
      you,
Whom Thackeray rated best of all our crew, —
Had letters kept you, every wreath were yours;
Had the World tempted, all its chariest doors
Had swung on flattered hinges to admit
Such high-bred manners, such good-natured wit;
At courts, in senates, who so fit to serve?
And both invited, but you would not swerve,
All meaner prizes waiving that you might
In civic duty spend your heat and light,
Unpaid, untrammelled, with a sweet disdain
Refusing posts men grovel to attain.
Good Man all own you; what is left me, then,
To heighten praise with but Good Citizen?

But why this praise to make you blush and stare,
And give a backache to your Easy-Chair?
Old Crestien rightly says no language can
Express the worth of a true Gentleman,
And I agree; but other thoughts deride
My first intent, and lure my pen aside.

Thinking of you, I see my firelight glow
On other faces, loved from long ago,
Dear to us both, and all these loves combine
With this I send and crowd in every line;
Fortune with me was in such generous mood
That all my friends were yours, and all were good;
Three generations come when one I call,
And the fair grandame, youngest of them all,
In her own Florida who found and sips
The fount that fled from Ponce's longing lips.
How bright they rise and wreathe my hearthstone
      round,
Divine my thoughts, reply without a sound,
And with them many a shape that memory sees,
As dear as they, but crowned with aureoles these!
What wonder if, with protest in my thought,
Arrived, I find 't was only love I brought?
I came with protest; Memory barred the road
Till I repaid you half the debt I owed.

No, 't was not to bring laurels that I came,
Nor would you wish it, daily seeing fame
(Or our cheap substitute, unknown of yore),
Dumped like a load of coal at every door,
Mime and hetæra getting equal weight
With him whose toils heroic saved the State.
But praise can harm not who so calmly met
Slander's worst word, nor treasured up the debt,
Knowing, what all experience serves to show,
No mud can soil us but the mud we throw.
You have heard harsher voices and more loud,
As all must, not sworn liegemen of the crowd,

And far aloof your silent mind could keep
As when, in heavens with winter-midnight deep,
The perfect moon hangs thoughtful, nor can know
What hounds her lucent calm drives mad below.

But to my business, while you rub your eyes
And wonder how you ever thought me wise.
Dear friend and old, they say you shake your head
And wish some bitter words of mine unsaid:
I wish they might be, — there we are agreed;
I hate to speak, still more what makes the need;
But I must utter what the voice within
Dictates, for acquiescence dumb were sin;
I blurt ungrateful truths, if so they be,
That none may need to say them after me.
'T were my felicity could I attain
The temperate zeal that balances your brain;
But nature still o'erleaps reflection's plan,
And one must do his service as he can.
Think you it were not pleasanter to speak
Smooth words that leave unflushed the brow and
      cheek?
To sit, well-dined, with cynic smile, unseen
In private box, spectator of the scene
Where men the comedy of life rehearse,
Idly to judge which better and which worse
Each hireling actor spoiled his worthless part?
Were it not sweeter with a careless heart,
In happy commune with the untainted brooks,
To dream all day, or, walled with silent books,
To hear nor heed the World's unmeaning noise,
Safe in my fortress stored with lifelong joys?

I love too well the pleasures of retreat
Safe from the crowd and cloistered from the
      street;
The fire that whispers its domestic joy,
Flickering on walls that knew me still a boy,
And knew my saintly father; the full days,
Not careworn from the world's soul-squandering
      ways,
Calm days that loiter with snow-silent tread,
Nor break my commune with the undying dead;
Truants of Time, to-morrow like to-day,
That come unbid, and claimless glide away
By shelves that sun them in the indulgent Past,
Where Spanish castles, even, were built to last,
Where saint and sage their silent vigil keep,
And wrong hath ceased or sung itself to sleep.
Dear were my walks, too, gathering fragrant store
Of Mother Nature's simple-minded lore:
I learned all weather-signs of day or night;
No bird but I could name him by his flight,
No distant tree but by his shape was known,
Or, near at hand, by leaf or bark alone.
This learning won by loving looks I hived
As sweeter lore than all from books derived.
I know the charm of hillside, field, and wood,
Of lake and stream, and the sky's downy brood,
Of roads sequestered rimmed with sallow sod,
But friends with hardhack, aster, goldenrod,
Or succory keeping summer long its trust
Of heaven-blue fleckless from the eddying dust:
These were my earliest friends, and latest too,
Still unestranged, whatever fate may do.

For years I had these treasures, knew their worth,
Estate most real man can have on earth.
I sank too deep in this soft-stuffed repose
That hears but rumors of earth's wrongs and
       woes;
Too well these Capuas could my muscles waste,
Not void of toils, but toils of choice and taste;
These still had kept me could I but have quelled
The Puritan drop that in my veins rebelled.
But there were times when silent were my books
As jailers are, and gave me sullen looks,
When verses palled, and even the woodland path,
By innocent contrast, fed my heart with wrath,
And I must twist my little gift of words
Into a scourge of rough and knotted cords
Unmusical, that whistle as they swing
To leave on shameless backs their purple sting.

How slow Time comes! Gone, who so swift as he?
Add but a year, 't is half a century
Since the slave's stifled moaning broke my sleep,
Heard 'gainst my will in that seclusion deep,
Haply heard louder for the silence there,
And so my fancied safeguard made my snare.
After that moan had sharpened to a cry,
And a cloud, hand-broad then, heaped all our sky
With its stored vengeance, and such thunders stirred
As heaven's and earth's remotest chambers heard,
I looked to see an ampler atmosphere
By that electric passion-gust blown clear.
I looked for this; consider what I see —
But I forbear, 't would please nor you nor me

To check the items in the bitter list
Of all I counted on and all I mist.
Only three instances I choose from all,
And each enough to stir a pigeon's gall:
Office a fund for ballot-brokers made
To pay the drudges of their gainful trade;
Our cities taught what conquered cities feel
By ædiles chosen that they might safely steal;
And gold, however got, a title fair
To such respect as only gold can bear.
I seem to see this; how shall I gainsay
What all our journals tell me every day?
Poured our young martyrs their high-hearted blood
That we might trample to congenial mud
The soil with such a legacy sublimed?
Methinks an angry scorn is here well-timed:
Where find retreat?   How keep reproach at bay?
Where'er I turn some scandal fouls the way.

Dear friend, if any man I wished to please,
'T were surely you whose humor's honied ease
Flows flecked with gold of thought, whose generous
          mind
Sees Paradise regained by all mankind,
Whose brave example still to vanward shines,
Checks the retreat, and spurs our lagging lines.
Was I too bitter?   Who his phrase can choose
That sees the life-blood of his dearest ooze?
I loved my Country so as only they
Who love a mother fit to die for may;
I loved her old renown, her stainless fame, —
What better proof than that I loathed her shame?

That many blamed me could not irk me long,
But, if you doubted, must I not be wrong?
'T is not for me to answer: this I know,
That man or race so prosperously low
Sunk in success that wrath they cannot feel,
Shall taste the spurn of parting Fortune's heel;
For never land long lease of empire won
Whose sons sate silent when base deeds were
      done.   .

POSTSCRIPT 1887

Curtis, so wrote I thirteen years ago,
Tost it unfinished by, and left it so;
Found lately, I have pieced it out, or tried,
Since time for callid juncture was denied.
Some of the verses pleased me, it is true,
And still were pertinent, — those honoring you.
These now I offer: take them, if you will,
Like the old hand-grasp, when at Shady Hill
We met, or Staten Island, in the days
When life was its own spur, nor needed praise.
If once you thought me rash, no longer fear;
Past my next milestone waits my seventieth year.
I mount no longer when the trumpets call;
My battle-harness idles on the wall,
The spider's castle, camping-ground of dust,
Not without dints, and all in front, I trust.
Shivering sometimes it calls me as it hears
Afar the charge's tramp and clash of spears;
But 't is such murmur only as might be
The sea-shell's lost tradition of the sea,

That makes me muse and wonder Where? and
        When?
While from my cliff I watch the waves of men
That climb to break midway their seeming gain,
And think it triumph if they shake their chain.
Little I ask of Fate; will she refuse
Some days of reconcilement with the Muse?
I take my reed again and blow it free
Of dusty silence, murmuring, " Sing to me ! "
And, as its stops my curious touch retries,
The stir of earlier instincts I surprise, —
Instincts, if less imperious, yet more strong,
And happy in the toil that ends with song.

Home am I come : not, as I hoped might be,
To the old haunts, too full of ghosts for me,
But to the olden dreams that time endears,
And the loved books that younger grow with years;
To country rambles, timing with my tread
Some happier verse that carols in my head,
Yet all with sense of something vainly mist,
Of something lost, but when I never wist.
How empty seems to me the populous street,
One figure gone I daily loved to meet, —
The clear, sweet singer with the crown of snow
Not whiter than the thoughts that housed below !
And, ah, what absence feel I at my side,
Like Dante when he missed his laurelled guide,
What sense of diminution in the air
Once so inspiring, Emerson not there !
But life is sweet, though all that makes it sweet
Lessen like sound of friends' departing feet,

And Death is beautiful as feet of friend
Coming with welcome at our journey's end;
For me Fate gave, whate'er she else denied,
A nature sloping to the southern side;
I thank her for it, though when clouds arise
Such natures double-darken gloomy skies.
I muse upon the margin of the sea,
Our common pathway to the new To Be,
Watching the sails, that lessen more and more,
Of good and beautiful embarked before;
With bits of wreck I patch the boat shall bear
Me to that unexhausted Otherwhere,
Whose friendly-peopled shore I sometimes see,
By soft mirage uplifted, beckon me,
Nor sadly hear, as lower sinks the sun,
My moorings to the past snap one by one.

SENTIMENT

ENDYMION

A MYSTICAL COMMENT ON TITIAN'S "SACRED AND
PROFANE LOVE"

I

My day began not till the twilight fell,
And, lo, in ether from heaven's sweetest well,
The New Moon swam divinely isolate
In maiden silence, she that makes my fate
Haply not knowing it, or only so
As I the secrets of my sheep may know;
Nor ask I more, entirely blest if she,
In letting me adore, ennoble me
To height of what the Gods meant making man,
As only she and her best beauty can.
Mine be the love that in itself can find
Seed of white thoughts, the lilies of the mind,
Seed of that glad surrender of the will
That finds in service self's true purpose still;
Love that in outward fairness sees the tent
Pitched for an inmate far more excellent;
Love with a light irradiate to the core,
Lit at her lamp, but fed from inborn store;
Love thrice-requited with the single joy
Of an immaculate vision naught could cloy,

Dearer because, so high beyond my scope,
My life grew rich with her, unbribed by hope
Of other guerdon save to think she knew
One grateful votary paid her all her due;
Happy if she, high-radiant there, resigned
To his sure trust her image in his mind.
O fairer even than Peace is when she comes
Hushing War's tumult, and retreating drums
Fade to a murmur like the sough of bees
Hidden among the noon-stilled linden-trees,
Bringer of quiet, thou that canst allay
The dust and din and travail of the day,
Strewer of Silence, Giver of the dew
That doth our pastures and our souls renew,
Still dwell remote, still on thy shoreless sea
Float unattained in silent empery,
Still light my thoughts, nor listen to a prayer
Would make thee less imperishably fair!

II

Can, then, my twofold nature find content
In vain conceits of airy blandishment?
Ask I no more? Since yesterday I task
My storm-strewn thoughts to tell me what I ask:
Faint premonitions of mutation strange
Steal o'er my perfect orb, and, with the change,
Myself am changed; the shadow of my earth
Darkens the disk of that celestial worth
Which only yesterday could still suffice
Upwards to waft my thoughts in sacrifice;
My heightened fancy with its touches warm
Moulds to a woman's that ideal form;

Nor yet a woman's wholly, but divine
With awe her purer essence bred in mine.
Was it long brooding on their own surmise,
Which, of the eyes engendered, fools the eyes,
Or have I seen through that translucent air
A Presence shaped in its seclusions bare,
My Goddess looking on me from above
As look our russet maidens when they love,
But high-uplifted o'er our human heat
And passion-paths too rough for her pearl feet?

Slowly the Shape took outline as I gazed
At her full-orbed or crescent, till, bedazed
With wonder-working light that subtly wrought
My brain to its own substance, steeping thought
In trances such as poppies give, I saw
Things shut from vision by sight's sober law,
Amorphous, changeful, but defined at last
Into the peerless Shape mine eyes hold fast.
This, too, at first I worshipt: soon, like wine,
Her eyes, in mine poured, frenzy-philtred mine;
Passion put Worship's priestly raiment on
And to the woman knelt, the Goddess gone.
Was I, then, more than mortal made? or she
Less than divine that she might mate with me?
If mortal merely, could my nature cope
With such o'ermastery of maddening hope?
If Goddess, could she feel the blissful woe
That women in their self-surrender know?

III

Long she abode aloof there in her heaven,
Far as the grape-bunch of the Pleiad seven
Beyond my madness' utmost leap; but here
Mine eyes have feigned of late her rapture near,
Moulded of mind-mist that broad day dispels,
Here in these shadowy woods and brook-lulled dells.

Have no heaven-habitants e'er felt a void
In hearts sublimed with ichor unalloyed ?
E'er longed to mingle with a mortal fate
Intense with pathos of its briefer date ?
Could she partake, and live, our human stains ?
Even with the thought there tingles through my veins
Sense of unwarned renewal; I, the dead,
Receive and house again the ardor fled,
As once Alcestis; to the ruddy brim
Feel masculine virtue flooding every limb,
And life, like Spring returning, brings the key
That sets my senses from their winter free,
Dancing like naked fauns too glad for shame.
Her passion, purified to palest flame,
Can it thus kindle ? Is her purpose this ?
I will not argue, lest I lose a bliss
That makes me dream Tithonus' fortune mine
(Or what of it was palpably divine
Ere came the fruitlessly immortal gift);
I cannot curb my hope's imperious drift
That wings with fire my dull mortality ;
Though fancy-forged, 't is all I feel or see.

v

IV

My Goddess sinks; round Latmos' darkening brow
Trembles the parting of her presence now,
Faint as the perfume left upon the grass
By her limbs' pressure or her feet that pass
By me conjectured, but conjectured so
As things I touch far fainter substance show.
Was it mine eyes' imposture I have seen
Flit with the moonbeams on from shade to sheen
Through the wood-openings? Nay, I see her now
Out of her heaven new-lighted, from her brow
The hair breeze-scattered, like loose mists that blow
Across her crescent, goldening as they go
High-kirtled for the chase, and what was shown,
Of maiden rondure, like the rose half-blown.
If dream, turn real! If a vision, stay!
Take mortal shape, my philtre's spell obey!
If hags compel thee from thy secret sky
With gruesome incantations, why not I,
Whose only magic is that I distil
A potion, blent of passion, thought, and will,
Deeper in reach, in force of fate more rich,
Than e'er was juice wrung by Thessalian witch
From moon-enchanted herbs, — a potion brewed
Of my best life in each diviner mood?
Myself the elixir am, myself the bowl
Seething and mantling with my soul of soul.
Taste and be humanized: what though the cup,
With thy lips frenzied, shatter? Drink it up!
If but these arms may clasp, o'erquited so,
My world, thy heaven, all life means I shall know.

V

Sure she hath heard my prayer and granted half,
As Gods do who at mortal madness laugh.
Yet if life's solid things illusion seem,
Why may not substance wear the mask of dream?
In sleep she comes; she visits me in dreams,
And, as her image in a thousand streams,
So in my veins, that her obey, she sees,
Floating and flaming there, her images
Bear to my little world's remotest zone
Glad messages of her, and her alone.
With silence-sandalled Sleep she comes to me
(But softer-footed, sweeter-browed, than she),
In motion gracious as a seagull's wing,
And all her bright limbs, moving, seem to sing.
Let me believe so, then, if so I may
With the night's bounty feed my beggared day.
In dreams I see her lay the goddess down
With bow and quiver, and her crescent-crown
Flicker and fade away to dull eclipse
As down to mine she deigns her longed-for lips;
And as her neck my happy arms enfold,
Flooded and lustred with her loosened gold,
She whispers words each sweeter than a kiss:
Then, wakened with the shock of sudden bliss,
My arms are empty, my awakener fled,
And, silent in the silent sky o'erhead,
But coldly as on ice-plated snow, she gleams,
Herself the mother and the child of dreams.

VI

Gone is the time when phantasms could appease
My quest phantasmal and bring cheated ease;
When, if she glorified my dreams, I felt
Through all my limbs a change immortal melt
At touch of hers illuminate with soul.
Not long could I be stilled with Fancy's dole;
Too soon the mortal mixture in me caught
Red fire from her celestial flame, and fought
For tyrannous control in all my veins:
My fool's prayer was accepted; what remains?
Or was it some eidolon merely, sent
By her who rules the shades in banishment,
To mock me with her semblance? Were it thus,
How 'scape I shame, whose will was traitorous?
What shall compensate an ideal dimmed?
How blanch again my statue virgin-limbed,
Soiled with the incense-smoke her chosen priest
Poured more profusely as within decreased
The fire unearthly, fed with coals from far
Within the soul's shrine? Could my fallen star
Be set in heaven again by prayers and tears
And quenchless sacrifice of all my years,
How would the victim to the flamen leap,
And life for life's redemption paid hold cheap!

But what resource when she herself descends
From her blue throne, and o'er her vassal bends
That shape thrice-deified by love, those eyes
Wherein the Lethe of all others lies?
When my white queen of heaven's remoteness
    tires,

Herself against her other self conspires,
Takes woman's nature, walks in mortal ways,
And finds in my remorse her beauty's praise?
Yet all would I renounce to dream again
The dream in dreams fulfilled that made my pain,
My noble pain that heightened all my years
With crowns to win and prowess-breeding tears;
Nay, would that dream renounce once more to see
Her from her sky there looking down at me!

VII

Goddess, reclimb thy heaven, and be once more
An inaccessible splendor to adore,
A faith, a hope of such transcendent worth
As bred ennobling discontent with earth;
Give back the longing, back the elated mood
That, fed with thee, spurned every meaner good;
Give even the spur of impotent despair
That, without hope, still bade aspire and dare;
Give back the need to worship, that still pours
Down to the soul the virtue it adores!

Nay, brightest and most beautiful, deem naught
These frantic words, the reckless wind of thought;
Still stoop, still grant, — I live but in thy will;
Be what thou wilt, but be a woman still!
Vainly I cried, nor could myself believe
That what I prayed for I would fain receive.
My moon is set; my vision set with her;
No more can worship vain my pulses stir.
Goddess Triform, I own thy triple spell,
My heaven's queen, — queen, too, of my earth and
        hell!

THE BLACK PREACHER

A BRETON LEGEND

At Carnac in Brittany, close on the bay,
They show you a church, or rather the gray
Ribs of a dead one, left there to bleach
With the wreck lying near on the crest of the beach,
Roofless and splintered with thunder-stone,
'Mid lichen-blurred gravestones all alone;
'T is the kind of ruin strange sights to see
That may have their teaching for you and me.

Something like this, then, my guide had to tell,
Perched on a saint cracked across when he fell;
But since I might chance give his meaning a wrench,
He talking his *patois* and I English-French,
I 'll put what he told me, preserving the tone,
In a rhymed prose that makes it half his, half my own.

An abbey-church stood here, once on a time,
Built as a death-bed atonement for crime:
'T was for somebody's sins, I know not whose;
But sinners are plenty, and you can choose.
Though a cloister now of the dusk-winged bat,
'T was rich enough once, and the brothers grew fat,
Looser in girdle and purpler in jowl,
Singing good rest to the founder's lost soul.
But one day came Northmen, and lithe tongues of fire

Lapped up the chapter-house, licked off the spire,
And left all a rubbish-heap, black and dreary,
Where only the wind sings *miserere*.

No priest has kneeled since at the altar's foot,
Whose crannies are searched by the nightshade's
      root,
Nor sound of service is ever heard,
Except from throat of the unclean bird,
Hooting to unassoiled shapes as they pass
In midnights unholy his witches' mass,
Or shouting " Ho ! ho ! " from the belfry high
As the Devil's sabbath-train whirls by.

But once a year, on the eve of All-Souls,
Through these arches dishallowed the organ rolls,
Fingers long fleshless the bell-ropes work,
The chimes peal muffled with sea-mists mirk,
The skeleton windows are traced anew
On the baleful flicker of corpse-lights blue,
And the ghosts must come, so the legend saith,
To a preaching of Reverend Doctor Death.

Abbots, monks, barons, and ladies fair
Hear the dull summons and gather there :
No rustle of silk now, no clink of mail,
Nor ever a one greets his church-mate pale;
No knight whispers love in the *châtelaine's* ear,
His next-door neighbor this five-hundred year ;
No monk has a sleek *benedicite*
For the great lord shadowy now as he;
Nor needeth any to hold his breath,
Lest he lose the least word of Doctor Death.

He chooses his text in the Book Divine,
Tenth verse of the Preacher in chapter nine : —
" ' Whatsoever thy hand shall find thee to do,
That do with thy whole might, or thou shalt rue ;
For no man is wealthy, or wise, or brave,
In that quencher of might-be's and would-be's,
the grave.'
Bid by the Bridegroom, ' To-morrow,' ye said,
And To-morrow was digging a trench for your
bed ;
Ye said, ' God can wait ; let us finish our wine ; '
Ye had wearied Him, fools, and that last knock
was mine ! ' "

But I can't pretend to give you the sermon,
Or say if the tongue were French, Latin, or Ger-
man ;
Whatever he preached in, I give you my word
The meaning was easy to all that heard ;
Famous preachers there have been and be,
But never was one so convincing as he ;
So blunt was never a begging friar,
No Jesuit's tongue so barbed with fire,
Cameronian never, nor Methodist,
Wrung gall out of Scripture with such a twist.

And would you know who his hearers must be ?
I tell you just what my guide told me :
Excellent teaching men have, day and night,
From two earnest friars, a black and a white,
The Dominican Death and the Carmelite Life ;

And between these two there is never strife,
For each has his separate office and station,
And each his own work in the congregation;
Whoso to the white brother deafens his ears,
And cannot be wrought on by blessings or tears,
Awake in his coffin must wait and wait,
In that blackness of darkness that means *too late*,
And come once a year, when the ghost-bell tolls,
As till Doomsday it shall on the eve of All-Souls,
To hear Doctor Death, whose words smart with
    the brine
Of the Preacher, the tenth verse of chapter nine.

ARCADIA REDIVIVA

I, WALKING the familiar street,
    While a crammed horse-car jingled through it,
Was lifted from my prosy feet
    And in Arcadia ere I knew it.

Fresh sward for gravel soothed my tread,
    And shepherd's pipes my ear delighted;
The riddle may be lightly read :
    I met two lovers newly plighted.

They murmured by in happy care,
    New plans for paradise devising,
Just as the moon, with pensive stare,
    O'er Mistress Craigie's pines was rising.

Astarte, known nigh threescore years,
    Me to no speechless rapture urges ;
Them in Elysium she enspheres,
    Queen, from of old, of thaumaturges.

The railings put forth bud and bloom,
    The house-fronts all with myrtles twine them,
And light-winged Loves in every room
    Make nests, and then with kisses line them.

O sweetness of untasted life !
    O dream, its own supreme fulfilment !
O hours with all illusion rife,
    As ere the heart divined what ill meant !

" *Et ego*," sighed I to myself,
    And strove some vain regrets to bridle,
" Though now laid dusty on the shelf,
    Was hero once of such an idyl !

" An idyl ever newly sweet,
    Although since Adam's day recited,
Whose measures time them to Love's feet,
    Whose sense is every ill requited."

Maiden, if I may counsel, drain
    Each drop of this enchanted season,
For even our honeymoons must wane,
    Convicted of green cheese by Reason.

And none will seem so safe from change,
    Nor in such skies benignant hover,
As this, beneath whose witchery strange
    You tread on rose-leaves with your lover.

The glass unfilled all tastes can fit,
 As round its brim Conjecture dances;
For not Mephisto's self hath wit
 To draw such vintages as Fancy's.

When our pulse beats its minor key, .
 When play-time halves and school-time
  doubles,
Age fills the cup with serious tea,
 Which once Dame Clicquot starred with
  bubbles.

" Fie, Mr. Graybeard ! Is this wise ?
 Is this the moral of a poet,
Who, when the plant of Eden dies,
 Is privileged once more to sow it ?

" That herb of clay-disdaining root,
 From stars secreting what it feeds on,
Is burnt-out passion's slag and soot
 Fit soil to strew its dainty seeds on ?

" Pray, why, if in Arcadia once,
 Need one so soon forget the way there ?
Or why, once there, be such a dunce
 As not contentedly to stay there ? "

Dear child, 't was but a sorry jest,
 And from my heart I hate the cynic
Who makes the Book of Life a nest
 For comments staler than rabbinic.

If Love his simple spell but keep,
    Life with ideal eyes to flatter,
The Grail itself were crockery cheap
    To Every-day's communion-platter.

One Darby is to me well known,
    Who, as the hearth between them blazes,
Sees the old moonlight shine on Joan,
    And float her youthward in its hazes.

He rubs his spectacles, he stares, —
    'T is the same face that witched him early!
He gropes for his remaining hairs, —
    Is this a fleece that feels so curly?

" Good heavens! but now 't was winter gray,
    And I of years had more than plenty;
The almanac 's a fool! 'T is May!
    Hang family Bibles! I am twenty!

" Come, Joan, your arm; we'll walk the room —
    The lane, I mean — do you remember?
How confident the roses bloom,
    As if it ne'er could be December!

" Nor more it shall, while in your eyes
    My heart its summer heat recovers,
And you, howe'er your mirror lies,
    Find your old beauty in your lover's."

THE NEST

MAY

WHEN oaken woods with buds are pink,
  And new-come birds each morning sing,
When fickle May on Summer's brink
  Pauses, and knows not which to fling,
Whether fresh bud and bloom again,
Or hoar-frost silvering hill and plain,

Then from the honeysuckle gray
  The oriole with experienced quest
Twitches the fibrous bark away,
  The cordage of his hammock-nest,
Cheering his labor with a note
Rich as the orange of his throat.

High o'er the loud and dusty road
  The soft gray cup in safety swings,
To brim ere August with its load
  Of downy breasts and throbbing wings,
O'er which the friendly elm-tree heaves
An emerald roof with sculptured eaves.

Below, the noisy World drags by
  In the old way, because it must,
The bride with heartbreak in her eye,
  The mourner following hated dust:
Thy duty, wingëd flame of Spring,
Is but to love, and fly, and sing.

Oh, happy life, to soar and sway
   Above the life by mortals led,
Singing the merry months away,
   Master, not slave of daily bread,
And, when the Autumn comes, to flee
Wherever sunshine beckons thee!

PALINODE — DECEMBER

Like some lorn abbey now, the wood
   Stands roofless in the bitter air;
In ruins on its floor is strewed
   The carven foliage quaint and rare,
And homeless winds complain along
The columned choir once thrilled with song.

And thou, dear nest, whence joy and praise
   The thankful oriole used to pour,
Swing'st empty while the north winds chase
   Their snowy swarms from Labrador:
But, loyal to the happy past,
I love thee still for what thou wast.

Ah, when the Summer graces flee
   From other nests more dear than thou,
And, where June crowded once, I see
   Only bare trunk and disleaved bough;
When springs of life that gleamed and gushed
Run chilled, and slower, and are hushed;

When our own branches, naked long,
   The vacant nests of Spring betray,
Nurseries of passion, love, and song
   That vanished as our year grew gray;
When Life drones o'er a tale twice told
O'er embers pleading with the cold, —

I 'll trust, that, like the birds of Spring,
   Our good goes not without repair,
But only flies to soar and sing
   Far off in some diviner air,
Where we shall find it in the calms
Of that fair garden 'neath the palms.

A YOUTHFUL EXPERIMENT IN ENGLISH HEXAMETERS

IMPRESSIONS OF HOMER

SOMETIMES come pauses of calm, when the rapt bard,
    holding his heart back,
Over his deep mind muses, as when o'er awe-stricken
    ocean
Poises a heapt cloud luridly, ripening the gale and the
    thunder;
Slow rolls onward the verse with a long swell heaving
    and swinging,
Seeming to wait till, gradually wid'ning from far-off
    horizons,

Piling the deeps up, heaping the glad-hearted surges
    before it,
Gathers the thought as a strong wind darkening and
    cresting the tumult.
Then every pause, every heave, each trough in the
    waves, has its meaning;
Full-sailed, forth like a tall ship steadies the theme,
    and around it,
Leaping beside it in glad strength, running in wild
    glee beyond it,
Harmonies billow exulting and floating the soul
    where it lists them,
Swaying the listener's fantasy hither and thither like
    driftweed.

BIRTHDAY VERSES

WRITTEN IN A CHILD'S ALBUM

'T was sung of old in hut and hall
How once a king in evil hour
Hung musing o'er his castle wall,
And, lost in idle dreams, let fall
Into the sea his ring of power.

Then, let him sorrow as he might,
And pledge his daughter and his throne
To who restored the jewel bright,
The broken spell would ne'er unite;
The grim old ocean held its own.

Those awful powers on man that wait,
On man, the beggar or the king,
To hovel bare or hall of state
A magic ring that masters fate
With each succeeding birthday bring.

Therein are set four jewels rare:
Pearl winter, summer's ruby blaze,
Spring's emerald, and, than all more fair,
Fall's pensive opal, doomed to bear
A heart of fire bedreamed with haze.

To him the simple spell who knows
The spirits of the ring to sway,
Fresh power with every sunrise flows,
And royal pursuivants are those
That fly his mandates to obey.

But he that with a slackened will
Dreams of things past or things to be,
From him the charm is slipping still,
And drops, ere he suspect the ill,
Into the inexorable sea.

ESTRANGEMENT

THE path from me to you that led,
    Untrodden long, with grass is grown,
Mute carpet that his lieges spread
    Before the Prince Oblivion
When he goes visiting the dead.

V

And who are they but who forget?
   You, who my coming could surmise
Ere any hint of me as yet
   Warned other ears and other eyes,
See the path blurred without regret.

But when I trace its windings sweet
   With saddened steps, at every spot
That feels the memory in my feet,
   Each grass-blade turns forget-me-not,
Where murmuring bees your name repeat.

PHŒBE

ERE pales in Heaven the morning star,
A bird, the loneliest of its kind,
Hears Dawn's faint footfall from afar
While all its mates are dumb and blind.

It is a wee sad-colored thing,
As shy and secret as a maid,
That, ere in choir the robins ring,
Pipes its own name like one afraid.

It seems pain-prompted to repeat
The story of some ancient ill,
But *Phœbe! Phœbe!* sadly sweet
Is all it says, and then is still.

It calls and listens. Earth and sky,
Hushed by the pathos of its fate,
Listen : no whisper of reply
Comes from its doom-dissevered mate.

Phœbe ! it calls and calls again,
And Ovid, could he but have heard,
Had hung a legendary pain
About the memory of the bird ;

A pain articulate so long
In penance of some mouldered crime
Whose ghost still flies the Furies' thong
Down the waste solitudes of time.

Waif of the young World's wonder-hour,
When gods found mortal maidens fair,
And will malign was joined with power
Love's kindly laws to overbear,

Like Progne, did it feel the stress
And coil of the prevailing words
Close round its being, and compress
Man's ampler nature to a bird's ?

One only memory left of all
The motley crowd of vanished scenes,
Hers, and vain impulse to recall
By repetition what it means.

Phœbe ! is all it has to say
In plaintive cadence o'er and o'er,
Like children that have lost their way,
And know their names, but nothing more.

Is it a type, since Nature's Lyre
Vibrates to every note in man,
Of that insatiable desire,
Meant to be so since life began?

I, in strange lands at gray of dawn,
Wakeful, have heard that fruitless plaint
Through Memory's chambers deep withdrawn
Renew its iterations faint.

So nigh! yet from remotest years
It summons back its magic, rife
With longings unappeased, and tears
Drawn from the very source of life.

DAS EWIG-WEIBLICHE

How was I worthy so divine a loss,
  Deepening my midnights, kindling all my morns?
Why waste such precious wood to make my cross,
  Such far-sought roses for my crown of thorns?

And when she came, how earned I such a gift?
  Why spend on me, a poor earth-delving mole,
The fireside sweetnesses, the heavenward lift,
  The hourly mercy, of a woman's soul?

Ah, did we know to give her all her right,
  What wonders even in our poor clay were done!
It is not Woman leaves us to our night,
  But our brute earth that grovels from her sun.

Our nobler cultured fields and gracious domes
   We whirl too oft from her who still shines on
To light in vain our caves and clefts, the homes
   Of night-bird instincts pained till she be gone.

Still must this body starve our souls with shade ;
   But when Death makes us what we were before,
Then shall her sunshine all our depths invade,
   And not a shadow stain heaven's crystal floor.

THE RECALL

COME back before the birds are flown,
Before the leaves desert the tree,
And, through the lonely alleys blown,
Whisper their vain regrets to me
Who drive before a blast more rude,
The plaything of my gusty mood,
In vain pursuing and pursued !

Nay, come although the boughs be bare,
Though snowflakes fledge the summer's nest,
And in some far Ausonian air
The thrush, your minstrel, warm his breast.
Come, sunshine's treasurer, and bring
To doubting flowers their faith in spring,
To birds and me the need to sing !

ABSENCE

SLEEP is Death's image, — poets tell us so;
But Absence is the bitter self of Death,
And, you away, Life's lips their red forego,
Parched in an air unfreshened by your breath.

Light of those eyes that made the light of mine,
Where shine you? On what happier fields and
        flowers?
Heaven's lamps renew their lustre less divine,
But only serve to count my darkened hours.

If with your presence went your image too,
That brain-born ghost my path would never cross
Which meets me now where'er I once met you,
Then vanishes, to multiply my loss.

MONNA LISA

SHE gave me all that woman can,
Nor her soul's nunnery forego,
A confidence that man to man
Without remorse can never show.

Rare art, that can the sense refine
Till not a pulse rebellious stirs,
And, since she never can be mine,
Makes it seem sweeter to be hers!

THE OPTIMIST

TURBID from London's noise and smoke,
Here I find air and quiet too:
Air filtered through the beech and oak,
Quiet by nothing harsher broke
Than wood-dove's meditative coo.

The Truce of God is here; the breeze
Sighs as men sigh relieved from care,
Or tilts as lightly in the trees
As might a robin: all is ease,
With pledge of ampler ease to spare.

Time, leaning on his scythe, forgets
To turn the hour-glass in his hand,
And all life's petty cares and frets,
Its teasing hopes and weak regrets,
Are still as that oblivious sand.

Repose fills all the generous space
Of undulant plain; the rook and crow
Hush; 't is as if a silent grace,
By Nature murmured, calmed the face
Of Heaven above and Earth below.

From past and future toils I rest,
One Sabbath pacifies my year;
I am the halcyon, this my nest;
And all is safely for the best
While the World's there and I am here.

So I turn Tory for the nonce,
And think the radical a bore,
Who cannot see, thick-witted dunce,
That what was good for people once
Must be as good forevermore.

Sun, sink no deeper down the sky;
Earth, never change this summer mood;
Breeze, loiter thus forever by,
Stir the dead leaf or let it lie;
Since I am happy, all is good.

MIDDLETON, August, 1884.

ON BURNING SOME OLD LETTERS

WITH what odorous woods and spices
Spared for royal sacrifices,
With what costly gums seld-seen,
Hoarded to embalm a queen,
With what frankincense and myrrh,
Burn these precious parts of her,
Full of life and light and sweetness
As a summer day's completeness,
Joy of sun and song of bird
Running wild in every word,
Full of all the superhuman
Grace and winsomeness of woman?

O'er these leaves her wrist has slid,
Thrilled with veins where fire is hid
'Neath the skin's pellucid veil,
Like the opal's passion pale;
This her breath has sweetened; this
Still seems trembling with the kiss
She half-ventured on my name,
Brow and cheek and throat aflame;
Over all caressing lies
Sunshine left there by her eyes;
From them all an effluence rare
With her nearness fills the air,
Till the murmur I half-hear
Of her light feet drawing near.

Rarest woods were coarse and rough,
Sweetest spice not sweet enough,
Too impure all earthly fire
For this sacred funeral-pyre;
These rich relics must suffice
For their own dear sacrifice.

Seek we first an altar fit
For such victims laid on it:
It shall be this slab brought home
In old happy days from Rome, —
Lazuli, once blest to line
Dian's inmost cell and shrine.
Gently now I lay them there,
Pure as Dian's forehead bare,
Yet suffused with warmer hue,
Such as only Latmos knew.

Fire I gather from the sun
In a virgin lens: 't is done!
Mount the flames, red, yellow, blue,
As her moods were shining through,
Of the moment's impulse born, —
Moods of sweetness, playful scorn,
Half defiance, half surrender,
More than cruel, more than tender,
Flouts, caresses, sunshine, shade,
Gracious doublings of a maid
Infinite in guileless art,
Playing hide-seek with her heart.

On the altar now, alas,
There they lie a crinkling mass,
Writhing still, as if with grief
Went the life from every leaf;
Then (heart-breaking palimpsest!)
Vanishing ere wholly guessed,
Suddenly some lines flash back,
Traced in lightning on the black,
And confess, till now denied,
All the fire they strove to hide.
What they told me, sacred trust,
Stays to glorify my dust,
There to burn through dust and damp
Like a mage's deathless lamp,
While an atom of this frame
Lasts to feed the dainty flame.

All is ashes now, but they
In my soul are laid away,

And their radiance round me hovers
Soft as moonlight over lovers,
Shutting her and me alone
In dream-Edens of our own;
First of lovers to invent
Love, and teach men what it meant.

THE PROTEST

I COULD not bear to see those eyes
On all with wasteful largess shine,
And that delight of welcome rise
Like sunshine strained through amber wine,
But that a glow from deeper skies,
From conscious fountains more divine,
Is (is it?) mine.

Be beautiful to all mankind,
As Nature fashioned thee to be;
'T would anger me did all not find
The sweet perfection that's in thee:
Yet keep one charm of charms behind, —
Nay, thou 'rt so rich, keep two or three
For (is it?) me!

THE PETITION

OH, tell me less or tell me more,
Soft eyes with mystery at the core,
That always seem to meet my own
Frankly as pansies fully grown,
Yet waver still 'tween no and yes!

So swift to cavil and deny,
Then parley with concessions shy,
Dear eyes, that make their youth be mine
And through my inmost shadows shine,
Oh, tell me more or tell me less!

FACT OR FANCY

IN town I hear, scarce wakened yet,
My neighbor's clock behind the wall
Record the day's increasing debt,
And *Cuckoo! Cuckoo!* faintly call.

Our senses run in deepening grooves,
Thrown out of which they lose their tact,
And consciousness with effort moves
From habit past to present fact.

So, in the country waked to-day,
I hear, unwitting of the change,
A cuckoo's throb from far away
Begin to strike, nor think it strange.

The sound creates its wonted frame:
My bed at home, the songster hid
Behind the wainscoting, — all came
As long association bid.

Then, half aroused, ere yet Sleep's mist
From the mind's uplands furl away,
To the familiar sound I list,
Disputed for by Night and Day.

I count to learn how late it is,
Until, arrived at thirty-four,
I question, " What strange world is this
Whose lavish hours would make me poor ? "

Cuckoo! Cuckoo! Still on it went,
With hints of mockery in its tone;
How could such hoards of time be spent
By one poor mortal's wit alone?

I have it! Grant, ye kindly Powers,
I from this spot may never stir,
If only these uncounted hours
May pass, and seem too short, with Her!

But who She is, her form and face,
These to the world of dream belong;
She moves through fancy's visioned space,
Unbodied, like the cuckoo's song.

AGRO–DOLCE

ONE kiss from all others prevents me,
And sets all my pulses astir,
And burns on my lips and torments me:
'T is the kiss that I fain would give her.

One kiss for all others requites·me,
Although it is never to be,
And sweetens my dreams and invites me:
'T is the kiss that she dare not give me.

Ah, could it be mine, it were sweeter
Than honey bees garner in dream,
Though its bliss on my lips were fleeter
Than a swallow's dip to the stream.

And yet, thus denied, it can never
In the prose of life vanish away;
O'er my lips it must hover forever,
The sunshine and shade of my day.

THE BROKEN TRYST

WALKING alone where we walked together,
When June was breezy and blue,
I watch in the gray autumnal weather
The leaves fall inconstant as you.

If a dead leaf startle behind me,
I think 't is your garment's hem,
And, oh, where no memory could find me,
Might I whirl away with them!

CASA SIN ALMA

RECUERDO DE MADRID

SILENCIOSO por la puerta
Voy de su casa desierta
Do siempre feliz entré,
Y la encuentro en vano abierta
Cual la boca de una muerta
Despues que el alma se fué.

A CHRISTMAS CAROL

FOR THE SUNDAY-SCHOOL CHILDREN OF THE CHURCH OF THE DISCIPLES

" WHAT means this glory round our feet,"
    The Magi mused, " more bright than morn ? "
And voices chanted clear and sweet,
    " To-day the Prince of Peace is born ! "

"What means that star," the Shepherds said,
  "That brightens through the rocky glen?"
And angels, answering overhead,
    Sang, "Peace on earth, good will to men!"

'T is eighteen hundred years and more
    Since those sweet oracles were dumb;
We wait for Him, like them of yore;
    Alas, He seems so slow to come!

But it was said, in words of gold
    No time or sorrow e'er shall dim,
That little children might be bold
    In perfect trust to come to Him.

All round about our feet shall shine
    A light like that the wise men saw,
If we our loving wills incline
    To that sweet Life which is the Law.

So shall we learn to understand
    The simple faith of shepherds then,
And, clasping kindly hand in hand,
    Sing, "Peace on earth, good will to men!"

And they who do their souls no wrong,
    But keep at eve the faith of morn,
Shall daily hear the angel-song,
    "To-day the Prince of Peace is born!"

MY PORTRAIT GALLERY

OFT round my hall of portraiture I gaze,
By Memory reared, the artist wise and holy,
From stainless quarries of deep-buried days.
There, as I muse in soothing melancholy,
Your faces glow in more than mortal youth,
Companions of my prime, now vanished wholly,
The loud, impetuous boy, the low-voiced maiden,
Now for the first time seen in flawless truth.
Ah, never master that drew mortal breath
Can match thy portraits, just and generous Death,
Whose brush with sweet regretful tints is laden!
Thou paintest that which struggled here below
Half understood, or understood for woe,
And with a sweet forewarning
Mak'st round the sacred front an aureole glow
Woven of that light that rose on Easter morning.

PAOLO TO FRANCESCA

I WAS with thee in Heaven: I cannot tell
If years or moments, so the sudden bliss,
When first we found, then lost, us in a kiss,
Abolished Time, abolished Earth and Hell,
Left only Heaven. Then from our blue there fell
The dagger's flash, and did not fall amiss,

v

For nothing now can rob my life of this, —
That once with thee in Heaven, all else is well.
Us, undivided when man's vengeance came,
God's half-forgives that doth not here divide;
And, were this bitter whirl-blast fanged with flame,
To me 't were summer, we being side by side:
This granted, I God's mercy will not blame,
For, given thy nearness, nothing is denied.

SONNET

SCOTTISH BORDER

As sinks the sun behind yon alien hills
Whose heather-purpled slopes, in glory rolled,
Flush all my thought with momentary gold,
What pang of vague regret my fancy thrills?
Here 't is enchanted ground the peasant tills,
Where the shy ballad dared its blooms unfold,
And memory's glamour makes new sights seem old
As when our life some vanished dream fulfils.
Yet not to thee belong these painless tears,
Land loved ere seen: before my darkened eyes,
From far beyond the waters and the years,
Horizons mute that wait their poet rise;
The stream before me fades and disappears,
And in the Charles the western splendor dies.

SONNET

ON BEING ASKED FOR AN AUTOGRAPH IN VENICE

AMID these fragments of heroic days
When thought met deed with mutual passion's leap,
There sits a Fame whose silent trump makes cheap
What short-lived rumor of ourselves we raise.
They had far other estimate of praise
Who stamped the signet of their souls so deep
In art and action, and whose memories keep
Their height like stars above our misty ways:
In this grave presence to record my name
Something within me hangs the head and shrinks.
Dull were the soul without some joy in fame;
Yet here to claim remembrance were, methinks,
Like him who, in the desert's awful frame,
Notches his cockney initials on the Sphinx.

THE DANCING-BEAR

FAR over Elf-land poets stretch their sway,
And win their dearest crowns beyond the goal
Of their own conscious purpose; they control
With gossamer threads wide-flown our fancy's play,
And so our action. On my walk to-day,

A wallowing bear begged clumsily his toll,
When straight a vision rose of Atta Troll,
And scenes ideal witched mine eyes away.
Merci, Mossieu! " the astonished bear-ward cried,
Grateful for thrice his hope to me, the slave
Of partial memory, seeing at his side
A bear immortal. The glad dole I gave
Was none of mine; poor Heine o'er the wide
Atlantic welter stretched it from his grave.

THE MAPLE

THE Maple puts her corals on in May,
While loitering frosts about the lowlands cling,
To be in tune with what the robins sing,
Plastering new log huts 'mid her branches gray;
But when the Autumn southward turns away,
Then in her veins burns most the blood of Spring,
And every leaf, intensely blossoming,
Makes the year's sunset pale the set of day.
O Youth unprescient, were it only so
With trees you plant, and in whose shade reclined,
Thinking their drifting blooms Fate's coldest snow,
You carve dear names upon the faithful rind,
Nor in that vernal stem the cross foreknow
That Age shall bear, silent, yet unresigned!

The Maple puts her corals on in May

NIGHT-WATCHES

WHILE the slow clock, as they were miser's gold,
Counts and recounts the mornward steps of Time,
The darkness thrills with conscience of each crime
By Death committed, daily grown more bold.
Once more the list of all my wrongs is told,
And ghostly hands stretch to me from my prime
Helpless farewells, as from an alien clime;
For each new loss redoubles all the old.
This morn 't was May; the blossoms were astir
With southern wind; but now the boughs are bent
With snow instead of birds, and all things freeze.
How much of all my past is dumb with her,
And of my future, too, for with her went
Half of that world I ever cared to please!

DEATH OF QUEEN MERCEDES

HERS all that Earth could promise or bestow, —
Youth, Beauty, Love, a crown, the beckoning years,
Lids never wet, unless with joyous tears,
A life remote from every sordid woe,
And by a nation's swelled to lordlier flow.
What lurking-place, thought we, for doubts or fears,
When, the day's swan, she swam along the cheers
Of the Alcalá, five happy months ago?

The guns were shouting Io Hymen then
That, on her birthday, now denounce her doom;
The same white steeds that tossed their scorn of men
To-day as proudly drag her to the tomb.
Grim jest of fate! Yet who dare call it blind,
Knowing what life is, what our humankind?

PRISON OF CERVANTES

SEAT of all woes? Though Nature's stern decree
The narrowing soul with narrowing dungeon bind,
Yet was his free of motion as the wind,
And held both worlds, of spirit and sense, in fee.
In charmed communion with his dual mind
He wandered Spain, himself both knight and hind,
Redressing wrongs he knew must ever be.
His humor wise could see life's long deceit,
Man's baffled aims, nor therefore both despise;
His knightly nature could ill fortune greet
Like an old friend. Whose ever such kind eyes
That pierced so deep, such scope, save his whose feet
By Avon ceased 'neath the same April's skies?

TO A LADY PLAYING ON THE CITHERN

So dreamy-soft the notes, so far away
They seem to fall, the horns of Oberon
Blow their faint Hunt's-up from the good-time gone;
Or, on a morning of long-withered May,

Larks tinkle unseen o'er Claudian arches gray,
That Romeward crawl from Dreamland; and anon
My fancy flings her cloak of Darkness on,
To vanish from the dungeon of To-day.
In happier times and scenes I seem to be,
And, as her fingers flutter o'er the strings,
The days return when I was young as she,
And my fledged thoughts began to feel their wings
With all Heaven's blue before them : Memory
Or Music is it such enchantment sings ?

THE EYE'S TREASURY

GOLD of the reddening sunset, backward thrown
In largess on my tall paternal trees,
Thou with false hope or fear didst never tease
His heart that hoards thee ; nor is childhood flown
From him whose life no fairer boon hath known
Than that what pleased him earliest still should please :
And who hath incomes safe from chance as these,
Gone in a moment, yet for life his own ?
All other gold is slave of earthward laws ;
This to the deeps of ether takes its flight,
And on the topmost leaves makes glorious pause
Of parting pathos ere it yield to night :
So linger, as from me earth's light withdraws,
Dear touch of Nature, tremulously bright !

PESSIMOPTIMISM

Ye little think what toil it was to build
A world of men imperfect even as this,
Where we conceive of Good by what we miss,
Of Ill by that wherewith best days are filled;
A world whose every atom is self-willed,
Whose corner-stone is propt on artifice,
Whose joy is shorter-lived than woman's kiss,
Whose wisdom hoarded is but to be spilled.
Yet this is better than a life of caves,
Whose highest art was scratching on a bone,
Or chipping toilsome arrowheads of flint;
Better, though doomed to hear while Cleon raves,
To see wit's want eterned in paint or stone,
And wade the drain-drenched shoals of daily print.

THE BRAKES

What countless years and wealth of brain were spent
To bring us hither from our caves and huts,
And trace through pathless wilds the deep-worn ruts
Of faith and habit, by whose deep indent
Prudence may guide if genius be not lent,
Genius, not always happy when it shuts
Its ears against the plodder's ifs and buts,
Hoping in one rash leap to snatch the event.

The coursers of the sun, whose hoofs of flame
Consume morn's misty threshold, are exact
As bankers' clerks, and all this star-poised frame,
One swerve allowed, were with convulsion rackt;
This world were doomed, should Dulness fail, to
      tame
Wit's feathered heels in the stern stocks of fact.

A FOREBODING

WHAT were the whole void world, if thou wert
    dead,
Whose briefest absence can eclipse my day,
And make the hours that danced with Time away
Drag their funereal steps with muffled head?
Through thee, meseems, the very rose is red,
From thee the violet steals its breath in May,
From thee draw life all things that grow not gray,
And by thy force the happy stars are sped.
Thou near, the hope of thee to overflow
Fills all my earth and heaven, as when in Spring,
Ere April come, the birds and blossoms know,
And grasses brighten round her feet to cling;
Nay, and this hope delights all Nature so
That the dumb turf I tread on seems to sing.

FANCY

UNDER THE OCTOBER MAPLES

WHAT mean these banners spread,
These paths with royal red
So gayly carpeted?
Comes there a prince to-day?
Such footing were too fine
For feet less argentine
Than Dian's own or thine,
Queen whom my tides obey.

Surely for thee are meant
These hues so orient
That with a sultan's tent
Each tree invites the sun;
Our Earth such homage pays,
So decks her dusty ways,
And keeps such holidays,
For one, and only one.

My brain shapes form and face,
Throbs with the rhythmic grace
And cadence of her pace
To all fine instincts true;
Her footsteps, as they pass,
Than moonbeams over grass
Fall lighter, — but, alas,
More insubstantial too!

LOVE'S CLOCK

A PASTORAL

DAPHNIS, *waiting.*

O Dryad feet,
Be doubly fleet,
Timed to my heart's expectant beat
While I await her!
" At four," vowed she;
'T is scarcely three,
Yet by *my* time it seems to be
A good hour later!

CHLOE

Bid me not stay!
Hear reason, pray!
'T is striking six! Sure never day
Was short as this is!

DAPHNIS

Reason nor rhyme
Is in the chime!
It can't be five; I 've scarce had time
To beg two kisses!

BOTH

Early or late,
When lovers wait,
And Love's watch gains, if Time a gait
So snail-like chooses,

Why should his feet
Become more fleet
Than cowards' are, when lovers meet
And Love's watch loses?

ELEANOR MAKES MACAROONS

LIGHT of triumph in her eyes,
Eleanor her apron ties;
As she pushes back her sleeves,
High resolve her bosom heaves.
Hasten, cook! impel the fire
To the pace of her desire;
As you hope to save your soul,
Bring a virgin casserole,
Brightest bring of silver spoons, —
Eleanor makes macaroons!

Almond-blossoms, now a-dance
In the smile of Southern France,
Leave your sport with sun and breeze,
Think of duty, not of ease;
Fashion, 'neath their jerkins brown,
Kernels white as thistledown,
Tiny cheeses made with cream
From the Galaxy's mid-stream,
Blanched in light of honeymoons, —
Eleanor makes macaroons!

Now for sugar, — nay, our plan
Tolerates no work of man.

Hurry, then, ye golden bees;
Fetch your clearest honey, please,
Garnered on a Yorkshire moor,
While the last larks sing and soar,
From the heather-blossoms sweet
Where sea-breeze and sunshine meet,
And the Augusts mask as Junes, —
Eleanor makes macaroons!

Next the pestle and mortar find,
Pure rock-crystal, — these to grind
Into paste more smooth than silk,
Whiter than the milkweed's milk:
Spread it on a rose-leaf, thus,
Cate to please Theocritus;
Then the fire with spices swell,
While, for her completer spell,
Mystic canticles she croons, —
Eleanor makes macaroons!

Perfect! and all this to waste
On a graybeard's palsied taste!
Poets so their verses write,
Heap them full of life and light,
And then fling them to the rude
Mumbling of the multitude.
Not so dire her fate as theirs,
Since her friend this gift declares
Choicest of his birthday boons, —
Eleanor's dear macaroons!

February 22, 1884.

TELEPATHY

" And how could you dream of meeting ? "
  Nay, how can you ask me, sweet ?
All day my pulse had been beating
  The tune of your coming feet.

And as nearer and ever nearer
  I felt the throb of your tread,
To be in the world grew dearer,
  And my blood ran rosier red.

Love called, and I could not linger,
  But sought the forbidden tryst,
As music follows the finger
  Of the dreaming lutanist.

And though you had said it and said it,
  " We must not be happy to-day,"
Was I not wiser to credit
  The fire in my feet than your Nay ?

Love called, and I could not linger

SCHERZO

When the down is on the chin
And the gold-gleam in the hair,
When the birds their sweethearts win
And champagne is in the air,
Love is here, and Love is there,
Love is welcome everywhere.

Summer's cheek too soon turns thin,
Days grow briefer, sunshine rare;
Autumn from his cannekin
Blows the froth to chase Despair:
Love is met with frosty stare,
Cannot house 'neath branches bare.

When new life is in the leaf
And new red is in the rose,
Though Love's Maytime be as brief
As a dragon-fly's repose,
Never moments come like those,
Be they Heaven or Hell: who knows?

All too soon comes Winter's grief,
Spendthrift Love's false friends turn foes;
Softly comes Old Age, the thief,
Steals the rapture, leaves the throes:
Love his mantle round him throws, —
" Time to say Good-bye; it snows."

"FRANCISCUS DE VERULAMIO SIC COGITAVIT"

That's a rather bold speech, my Lord Bacon,
　For, indeed, is 't so easy to know
Just how much we from others have taken,
　And how much our own natural flow?

Since your mind bubbled up at its fountain,
　How many streams made it elate,
While it calmed to the plain from the mountain,
　As every mind must that grows great?

While you thought 't was You thinking as newly
　As Adam still wet with God's dew,
You forgot in your self-pride that truly
　The whole Past was thinking through you.

Greece, Rome, nay, your namesake, old Roger,
　With Truth's nameless delvers who wrought
In the dark mines of Truth, helped to prod your
　Fine brain with the goad of their thought.

As mummy was prized for a rich hue
　The painter no elsewhere could find,
So 't was buried men's thinking with which you
　Gave the ripe mellow tone to your mind.

I heard the proud strawberry saying,
　" Only look what a ruby I 've made ! "
It forgot how the bees in their maying
　Had brought it the stuff for its trade.

And yet there 's the half of a truth in it,
   And my Lord might his copyright sue;
For a thought 's his who kindles new youth in it,
   Or so puts it as makes it more true.

The birds but repeat without ending
   The same old traditional notes,
Which some, by more happily blending,
   Seem to make over new in their throats;

And we men through our old bit of song run,
   Until one just improves on the rest,
And we call a thing his, in the long run,
   Who utters it clearest and best.

AUSPEX

My heart, I cannot still it,
Nest that had song-birds in it;
And when the last shall go,
The dreary days, to fill it,
Instead of lark or linnet,
Shall whirl dead leaves and snow.

Had they been swallows only,
Without the passion stronger
That skyward longs and sings, —
Woe 's me, I shall be lonely
When I can feel no longer
The impatience of their wings!

V

A moment, sweet delusion,
Like birds the brown leaves hover;
But it will not be long
Before their wild confusion
Fall wavering down to cover
The poet and his song.

THE PREGNANT COMMENT

OPENING one day a book of mine,
I absent, Hester found a line
Praised with a pencil-mark, and this
She left transfigured with a kiss.

When next upon the page I chance,
Like Poussin's nymphs my pulses dance,
And whirl my fancy where it sees
Pan piping 'neath Arcadian trees,
Whose leaves no winter-scenes rehearse,
Still young and glad as Homer's verse.
" What mean," I ask, " these sudden joys ?
This feeling fresher than a boy's ?
What makes this line, familiar long,
New as the first bird's April song ?
I could, with sense illumined thus,
Clear doubtful texts in Æschylus ! "

Laughing, one day she gave the key,
My riddle's open-sesame ;
Then added, with a smile demure,
Whose downcast lids veiled triumph sure,

" If what I left there give you pain,
  You — you — can take it off again ;
  'T was for *my* poet, not for him,
  Your Doctor Donne there ! "

                          Earth grew dim
And wavered in a golden mist,
As rose, not paper, leaves I kissed.
Donne, you forgive ? I let you keep
Her precious comment, poet deep.

THE LESSON

I SAT and watched the walls of night
With cracks of sudden lightning glow,
And listened while with clumsy might
The thunder wallowed to and fro.

The rain fell softly now ; the squall,
That to a torrent drove the trees,
Had whirled beyond us to let fall
Its tumult on the whitening seas.

But still the lightning crinkled keen,
Or fluttered fitful from behind
The leaden drifts, then only seen,
That rumbled eastward on the wind.

Still as gloom followed after glare,
While bated breath the pine-trees drew,
Tiny Salmoneus of the air,
His mimic bolts the firefly threw.

He thought, no doubt, " Those flashes grand,
That light for leagues the shuddering sky,
Are made, a fool could understand,
By some superior kind of fly.

" He 's of our race's elder branch,
His family-arms the same as ours,
Both born the twy-forked flame to launch,
Of kindred, if unequal, powers."

And is man wiser ? Man who takes
His consciousness the law to be
Of all beyond his ken, and makes
God but a bigger kind of Me ?

SCIENCE AND POETRY

HE who first stretched his nerves of subtile wire
Over the land and through the sea-depths still,
Thought only of the flame-winged messenger
As a dull drudge that should encircle earth
With sordid messages of Trade, and tame
Blithe Ariel to a bagman. But the Muse
Not long will be defrauded. From her foe
Her misused wand she snatches ; at a touch,

The Age of Wonder is renewed again,
And to our disenchanted day restores
The Shoes of Swiftness that give odds to
      Thought,
The Cloak that makes invisible ; and with these
I glide, an airy fire, from shore to shore,
Or from my Cambridge whisper to Cathay.

A NEW YEAR'S GREETING

THE century numbers fourscore years ;
You, fortressed in your teens,
To Time's alarums close your ears,
And, while he devastates your peers,
Conceive not what he means.

If e'er life's winter fleck with snow
Your hair's deep shadowed bowers,
That winsome head an art would know
To make it charm, and wear it so
As 't were a wreath of flowers.

If to such fairies years must come,
May yours fall soft and slow
As, shaken by a bee's low hum,
The rose-leaves waver, sweetly dumb,
Down to their mates below !

THE DISCOVERY

I watched a moorland torrent run
Down through the rift itself had made,
Golden as honey in the sun,
Of darkest amber in the shade.

In this wild glen at last, methought,
The magic's secret I surprise;
Here Celia's guardian fairy caught
The changeful splendors of her eyes.

All else grows tame, the sky's one blue,
The one long languish of the rose,
But these, beyond prevision new,
Shall charm and startle to the close.

WITH A SEASHELL

Shell, whose lips, than mine more cold,
Might with Dian's ear make bold,
Seek my Lady's; if thou win
To that portal, shut from sin,
Where commissioned angels' swords
Startle back unholy words,
Thou a miracle shalt see
Wrought by it and wrought in thee;

Thou, the dumb one, shalt recover
Speech of poet, speech of lover.
If she deign to lift you there,
Murmur what I may not dare;
In that archway, pearly-pink
As the Dawn's untrodden brink,
Murmur, " Excellent and good,
Beauty's best in every mood,
Never common, never tame,
Changeful fair as windwaved flame — "
Nay, I maunder; this she hears
Every day with mocking ears,
With a brow not sudden-stained
With the flush of bliss restrained,
With no tremor of the pulse
More than feels the dreaming dulse
In the midmost ocean's caves,
When a tempest heaps the waves.
Thou must woo her in a phrase
Mystic as the opal's blaze,
Which pure maids alone can see
When their lovers constant be.
I with thee a secret share,
Half a hope, and half a prayer,
Though no reach of mortal skill
Ever told it all, or will;
Say, " He bids me — nothing more —
Tell you what you guessed before ! "

THE SECRET

I HAVE a fancy: how shall I bring it
Home to all mortals wherever they be?
Say it or sing it? Shoe it or wing it,
So it may outrun or outfly ME,
Merest cocoon-web whence it broke free?

Only one secret can save from disaster,
Only one magic is that of the Master:
Set it to music; give it a tune, —
Tune the brook sings you, tune the breeze brings
　　　　you,
Tune the wild columbines nod to in June!

This is the secret: so simple, you see!
Easy as loving, easy as kissing,
Easy as — well, let me ponder — as missing,
Known, since the world was, by scarce two or
　　　　three.

HUMOR AND SATIRE

FITZ ADAM'S STORY

[The greater part of this poem was written many years ago as part of a larger one, to be called "The Nooning," made up of tales in verse, some of them grave, some comic. It gives me a sad pleasure to remember that I was encouraged in this project by my friend the late Arthur Hugh Clough.]

THE next whose fortune 't was a tale to tell
Was one whom men, before they thought, loved
   well,
And after thinking wondered why they did,
For half he seemed to let them, half forbid,
And wrapped him so in humors, sheath on sheath,
'T was hard to guess the mellow soul beneath;
But, once divined, you took him to your heart,
While he appeared to bear with you as part
Of life's impertinence, and once a year
Betrayed his true self by a smile or tear,
Or rather something sweetly-shy and loath,
Withdrawn ere fully shown, and mixed of both.
A cynic? Not precisely: one who thrust
Against a heart too prone to love and trust,
Who so despised false sentiment he knew
Scarce in himself to part the false and true,
And strove to hide, by roughening-o'er the skin,
Those cobweb nerves he could not dull within.
Gentle by birth, but of a stem decayed,

He shunned life's rivalries and hated trade;
On a small patrimony and larger pride,
He lived uneaseful on the Other Side
(So he called Europe), only coming West
To give his Old-World appetite new zest;
Yet still the New World spooked it in his veins,
A ghost he could not lay with all his pains;
For never Pilgrims' offshoot scapes control
Of those old instincts that have shaped his soul.
A radical in thought, he puffed away
With shrewd contempt the dust of usage gray,
Yet loathed democracy as one who saw,
In what he longed to love, some vulgar flaw,
And, shocked through all his delicate reserves,
Remained a Tory by his taste and nerves.
His fancy's thrall, he drew all ergoes thence,
And thought himself the type of common sense;
Misliking women, not from cross or whim,
But that his mother shared too much in him,
And he half felt that what in them was grace
Made the unlucky weakness of his race.
What powers he had he hardly cared to know,
But sauntered through the world as through a show;
A critic fine in his haphazard way,
A sort of mild La Bruyère on half-pay.
For comic weaknesses he had an eye
Keen as an acid for an alkali,
Yet you could feel, through his sardonic tone,
He loved them all, unless they were his own.
You might have called him, with his humorous twist,
A kind of human entomologist:
As these bring home, from every walk they take,

Their hat-crowns stuck with bugs of curious make,
So he filled all the lining of his head
With characters impaled and ticketed,
And had a cabinet behind his eyes
For all they caught of mortal oddities.
He might have been a poet — many worse —
But that he had, or feigned, contempt of verse;
Called it tattooing language, and held rhymes
The young world's lullaby of ruder times.
Bitter in words, too indolent for gall,
He satirized himself the first of all,
In men and their affairs could find no law,
And was the ill logic that he thought he saw.

Scratching a match to light his pipe anew,
With eyes half-shut some musing whiffs he drew,
And thus began : "I give you all my word,
I think this mock-Decameron absurd;
Boccaccio's garden ! how bring that to pass
In our bleak clime save under double glass ?
The moral east-wind of New England life
Would snip its gay luxuriance like a knife;
Mile-deep the glaciers brooded here, they say,
Through æons numb; we feel their chill to-day.
These foreign plants are but half-hardy still,
Die on a south, and on a north wall chill.
Had we stayed Puritans ! *They* had some heat
(Though whence derived I have my own conceit),
But you have long ago raked up their fires;
Where they had faith, you 've ten sham-Gothic spires.
Why more exotics ? Try your native vines,
And in some thousand years you *may* have wines;

Your present grapes are harsh, all pulps and skins,
And want traditions of ancestral bins
That saved for evenings round the polished board
Old lava-fires, the sun-steeped hillside's hoard.
Without a Past, you lack that southern wall
O'er which the vines of Poesy should crawl;
Still they 're your only hope; no midnight oil
Makes up for virtue wanting in the soil;
Manure them well and prune them; 't won't be
    France,
Nor Spain, nor Italy, but there 's your chance.
You have one story-teller worth a score
Of dead Boccaccios, — nay, add twenty more, —
A hawthorn asking spring's most dainty breath,
And him you 're freezing pretty well to death.
However, since you say so, I will tease
My memory to a story by degrees,
Though you will cry, 'Enough!' I 'm well-nigh
    sure,
Ere I have dreamed through half my overture.
Stories were good for men who had no books
(Fortunate race!) and built their nests like rooks
In lonely towers, to which the Jongleur brought
His pedler's-box of cheap and tawdry thought,
With here and there a fancy fit to see
Wrought to quaint grace in golden filigree, —
Some ring that with the Muse's finger yet
Is warm, like Aucassin and Nicolete;
The morning newspaper has spoilt his trade
(For better or for worse, I leave unsaid),
And stories now, to suit a public nice,
Must be half epigram, half pleasant vice.

" All tourists know Shebagog County : there
The summer idlers take their yearly stare,
Dress to see Nature in a well-bred way,
As 't were Italian opera, or play,
Encore the sunrise (if they 're out of bed),
And pat the Mighty Mother on the head :
These have I seen, — all things are good to see, —
And wondered much at their complacency.
This world's great show, that took in getting-up
Millions of years, they finish ere they sup ;
Sights that God gleams through with soul-tingling
       force
They glance approvingly as things of course,
Say, ' That 's a grand rock,' ' This a pretty fall,'
Not thinking, ' Are we worthy ? ' What if all
The scornful landscape should turn round and say,
' This is a fool, and that a popinjay ' ?
I often wonder what the Mountain thinks
Of French boots creaking o'er his breathless brinks,
Or how the Sun would scare the chattering crowd,
If some fine day he chanced to think aloud.
I, who love Nature much as sinners can,
Love her where she most grandeur shows, — in man :
Here find I mountain, forest, cloud, and sun,
River and sea, and glows when day is done ;
Nay, where she makes grotesques, and moulds in jest
The clown's cheap clay, I find unfading zest.
The natural instincts year by year retire,
As deer shrink northward from the settler's fire,
And he who loves the wild game-flavor more
Than city-feasts, where every man 's a bore
To every other man, must seek it where

The steamer's throb and railway's iron blare
Have not yet startled with their punctual stir
The shy, wood-wandering brood of Character.

" There is a village, once the county town,
Through which the weekly mail rolled dustily
      down,
Where the courts sat, it may be, twice a year,
And the one tavern reeked with rustic cheer ;
Cheeshogquesumscot erst, now Jethro hight,
Red-man and pale-face bore it equal spite.
The railway ruined it, the natives say,
That passed unwisely fifteen miles away,
And made a drain to which, with steady ooze,
Filtered away law, stage-coach, trade, and news.
The railway saved it ; so at least think those
Who love old ways, old houses, old repose.
Of course the Tavern stayed : its genial host
Thought not of flitting more than did the post
On which high-hung the fading signboard creaks,
Inscribed, ' The Eagle Inn, by Ezra Weeks.'

" If in life's journey you should ever find
An inn medicinal for body and mind,
'T is sure to be some drowsy-looking house
Whose easy landlord has a bustling spouse :
He, if he like you, will not long forego
Some bottle deep in cobwebbed dust laid low,
That, since the War we used to call the ' Last,'
Has dozed and held its lang-syne memories fast ;
From him exhales that Indian-summer air
Of hazy, lazy welcome everywhere,

While with her toil the napery is white,
The china dustless, the keen knife-blades bright,
Salt dry as sand, and bread that seems as though
'T were rather sea-foam baked than vulgar dough.

" In our swift country, houses trim and white
Are pitched like tents, the lodging of a night;
Each on its bank of baked turf mounted high
Perches impatient o'er the roadside dry,
While the wronged landscape coldly stands aloof,
Refusing friendship with the upstart roof.
Not so the Eagle; on a grass-green swell
That toward the south with sweet concessions fell
It dwelt retired, and half had grown to be
As aboriginal as rock or tree.
It nestled close to earth, and seemed to brood
O'er homely thoughts in a half-conscious mood,
As by the peat that rather fades than burns
The smouldering grandam nods and knits by turns,
Happy, although her newest news were old
Ere the first hostile drum at Concord rolled.
If paint it e'er had known, it knew no more
Than yellow lichens spattered thickly o'er
That soft lead-gray, less dark beneath the eaves
Which the slow brush of wind and weather leaves.
The ample roof sloped backward to the ground,
And vassal lean-tos gathered thickly round,
Patched on, as sire or son had felt the need,
Like chance growths sprouting from the old roof's
        seed,
Just as about a yellow-pine-tree spring
Its rough-barked darlings in a filial ring.

But the great chimney was the central thought
Whose gravitation through the cluster wrought;
For 't is not styles far-fetched from Greece or Rome,
But just the Fireside, that can make a home;
None of your spindling things of modern style,
Like pins stuck through to stay the card-built pile,
It rose broad-shouldered, kindly, debonair,
Its warm breath whitening in the October air,
While on its front a heart in outline showed
The place it filled in that serene abode.

" When first I chanced the Eagle to explore,
Ezra sat listless by the open door;
One chair careened him at an angle meet,
Another nursed his hugely-slippered feet;
Upon a third reposed a shirt-sleeved arm,
And the whole man diffused tobacco's charm.
' Are you the landlord?' 'Wahl, I guess I be,'
Watching the smoke, he answered leisurely.
He was a stoutish man, and through the breast
Of his loose shirt there showed a brambly chest;
Streaked redly as a wind-foreboding morn,
His tanned cheeks curved to temples closely shorn;
Clean-shaved he was, save where a hedge of gray
Upon his brawny throat leaned every way
About an Adam's-apple, that beneath
Bulged like a boulder from a brambly heath.
The Western World's true child and nursling he,
Equipt with aptitudes enough for three:
No eye like his to value horse or cow,
Or gauge the contents of a stack or mow;
He could foretell the weather at a word,
He knew the haunt of every beast and bird,

Or where a two-pound trout was sure to lie,
Waiting the flutter of his home-made fly;
Nay, once in autumns five, he had the luck
To drop at fair-play range a ten-tined buck;
Of sportsmen true he favored every whim,
But never cockney found a guide in him;
A natural man, with all his instincts fresh,
Not buzzing helpless in Reflection's mesh,
Firm on its feet stood his broad-shouldered mind,
As bluffly honest as a northwest wind;
Hard-headed and soft-hearted, you 'd scarce meet
A kindlier mixture of the shrewd and sweet;
Generous by birth, and ill at saying ' No,'
Yet in a bargain he was all men's foe,
Would yield no inch of vantage in a trade,
And give away ere nightfall all he made.

" ' Can I have lodging here ? ' once more I said.
He blew a whiff, and, leaning back his head,
' You come a piece through Bailey's woods, I s'pose,
Acrost a bridge where a big swamp-oak grows?
It don't grow, neither; it 's ben dead ten year,
Nor th' ain't a livin' creetur, fur nor near,
Can tell wut killed it; but I some misdoubt
'T was borers, there 's sech heaps on 'em about.
You did n' chance to run ag'inst my son,
A long, slab-sided youngster with a gun?
He 'd ough' to ben back more 'n an hour ago,
An' brought some birds to dress for supper — sho!
There he comes now. 'Say, Obed, wut ye got?
(He 'll hev some upland plover like as not.)
Wal, them 's real nice uns, an' 'll eat A 1,

v

Ef I can stop their bein' over-done;
Nothin' riles *me* (I pledge my fastin' word)
Like cookin' out the natur' of a bird
(Obed, you pick 'em out o' sight an' sound,
Your ma'am don't love no feathers cluttrin' round);
Jes' scare 'em with the coals, — thet's *my* idee.'
Then, turning suddenly about on me,
' Wal, Square, I guess so. Calllate to stay?
I 'll ask Mis' Weeks; 'bout *thet* it 's hern to say.'

" Well, there I lingered all October through,
In that sweet atmosphere of hazy blue,
So leisurely, so soothing, so forgiving,
That sometimes makes New England fit for living.
I watched the landscape, erst so granite glum,
Bloom like the south side of a ripening plum,
And each rock-maple on the hillside make
His ten days' sunset doubled in the lake;
The very stone walls draggling up the hills
Seemed touched, and wavered in their roundhead wills.
Ah! there 's a deal of sugar in the sun!
Tap me in Indian summer, I should run
A juice to make rock-candy of, — but then
We get such weather scarce one year in ten.

" There was a parlor in the house, a room
To make you shudder with its prudish gloom.
The furniture stood round with such an air,
There seemed an old maid's ghost in every chair,
Which looked as it had scuttled to its place
And pulled extempore a Sunday face,
Too smugly proper for a world of sin,
Like boys on whom the minister comes in.

The table, fronting you with icy stare,
Strove to look witless that its legs were bare,
While the black sofa with its horse-hair pall
Gloomed like a bier for Comfort's funeral.
Each piece appeared to do its chilly best
To seem an utter stranger to the rest,
As if acquaintanceship were deadly sin,
Like Britons meeting in a foreign inn.
Two portraits graced the wall in grimmest truth,
Mister and Mistress W. in their youth, —
New England youth, that seems a sort of pill,
Half wish-I-dared, half Edwards on the Will,
Bitter to swallow, and which leaves a trace
Of Calvinistic colic on the face.
Between them, o'er the mantel, hung in state
Solomon's temple, done in copperplate;
Invention pure, but meant, we may presume,
To give some Scripture sanction to the room.
Facing this last, two samplers you might see,
Each, with its urn and stiffly-weeping tree,
Devoted to some memory long ago
More faded than their lines of worsted woe;
Cut paper decked their frames against the flies,
Though none e'er dared an entrance who were
          wise,
And bushed asparagus in fading green
Added its shiver to the franklin clean.

  "When first arrived, I chilled a half-hour there,
Nor dared deflower with use a single chair;
I caught no cold, yet flying pains could find
For weeks in me, — a rheumatism of mind.

One thing alone imprisoned there had power
To hold me in the place that long half-hour:
A scutcheon this, a helm-surmounted shield,
Three griffins argent on a sable field;
A relic of the shipwrecked past was here,
And Ezra held some Old-World lumber dear.
Nay, do not smile; I love this kind of thing,
These cooped traditions with a broken wing,
This freehold nook in Fancy's pipe-blown ball,
This less than nothing that is more than all!
Have I not seen sweet natures kept alive
Amid the humdrum of your business hive,
Undowered spinsters shielded from all harms,
By airy incomes from a coat of arms?"

He paused a moment, and his features took
The flitting sweetness of that inward look
I hinted at before; but, scarcely seen,
It shrank for shelter 'neath his harder mien,
And, rapping his black pipe of ashes clear,
He went on with a self-derisive sneer:
"No doubt we make a part of God's design,
And break the forest-path for feet divine;
To furnish foothold for this grand prevision
Is good, and yet — to be the mere transition,
That, you will say, is also good, though I
Scarce like to feed the ogre By-and-by.
Raw edges rasp my nerves; my taste is wooed
By things that are, not going to be, good,
Though were I what I dreamed two lustres gone,
I'd stay to help the Consummation on,
Whether a new Rome than the old more fair,
Or a deadflat of rascal-ruled despair;

But *my* skull somehow never closed the suture
That seems to knit yours firmly with the future,
So you 'll excuse me if I 'm sometimes fain
To tie the Past's warm nightcap o'er my brain;
I 'm quite aware 't is not in fashion here,
But then your northeast winds are *so* severe!

" But to my story: though 't is truly naught
But a few hints in Memory's sketch-book caught,
And which may claim a value on the score
Of calling back some scenery now no more.
Shall I confess? The tavern's only Lar
Seemed (be not shocked!) its homely-featured bar.
Here dozed a fire of beechen logs, that bred
Strange fancies in its embers golden-red,
And nursed the loggerhead whose hissing dip,
Timed by nice instinct, creamed the mug of flip
That made from mouth to mouth its genial
          round,
Nor left one nature wholly winter-bound;
Hence dropt the tinkling coal all mellow-ripe
For Uncle Reuben's talk-extinguished pipe;
Hence rayed the heat, as from an indoor sun,
That wooed forth many a shoot of rustic fun.
Here Ezra ruled as king by right divine;
No other face had such a wholesome shine,
No laugh like his so full of honest cheer;
Above the rest it crowed like Chanticleer.

" In this one room his dame you never saw,
Where reigned by custom old a Salic law;
Here coatless lolled he on his throne of oak,
And every tongue paused midway if he spoke.

Due mirth he loved, yet was his sway severe;
No blear-eyed driveller got his stagger here;
' Measure was happiness; who wanted more,
Must buy his ruin at the Deacon's store.'
None but his lodgers after ten could stay,
Nor after nine on eves of Sabbath-day.
He had his favorites and his pensioners,
The same that gypsy Nature owns for hers:
Loose-ended souls, whose skills bring scanty gold,
And whom the poor-house catches when they 're
    old;
Rude country-minstrels, men who doctor kine,
Or graft, and, out of scions ten, save nine;
Creatures of genius they, but never meant
To keep step with the civic regiment.
These Ezra welcomed, feeling in his mind
Perhaps some motions of the vagrant kind;
These paid no money, yet for them he drew
Special Jamaica from a tap they knew,
And, for their feelings, chalked behind the door
With solemn face a visionary score.
This thawed to life in Uncle Reuben's throat
A torpid shoal of jest and anecdote,
Like those queer fish that doze the droughts away,
And wait for moisture, wrapt in sun-baked clay;
This warmed the one-eyed fiddler to his task,
Perched in the corner on an empty cask,
By whose shrill art rapt suddenly, some boor
Rattled a double-shuffle on the floor;
' Hull's Victory ' was, indeed, the favorite air,
Though ' Yankee Doodle ' claimed its proper
    share.

"'T was there I caught from Uncle Reuben's lips,
In dribbling monologue 'twixt whiffs and sips,
The story I so long have tried to tell;
The humor coarse, the persons common, — well,
From Nature only do I love to paint,
Whether she send a satyr or a saint;
To me Sincerity 's the one thing good,
Soiled though she be and lost to maidenhood.
Quompegan is a town some ten miles south
From Jethro, at Nagumscot river-mouth,
A seaport town, and makes its title good
With lumber and dried fish and Eastern wood.
Here Deacon Bitters dwelt and kept the Store,
The richest man for many a mile of shore;
In little less than everything dealt he,
From meeting-houses to a chest of tea;
So dextrous therewithal a flint to skin,
He could make profit on a single pin;
In business strict, to bring the balance true
He had been known to bite a fig in two,
And change a board-nail for a shingle-nail.
All that he had he ready held for sale,
His house, his tomb, whate'er the law allows,
And he had gladly parted with his spouse.
His one ambition still to get and get,
He would arrest your very ghost for debt.
His store looked righteous, should the Parson come,
But in a dark back-room he peddled rum,
And eased Ma'am Conscience, if she e'er would scold,
By christening it with water ere he sold.
A small, dry man he was, who wore a queue,
And one white neckcloth all the week-days through, —

On Monday white, by Saturday as dun
As that worn homeward by the prodigal son.
His frosted earlocks, striped with foxy brown,
Were braided up to hide a desert crown;
His coat was brownish, black perhaps of yore;
In summer-time a banyan loose he wore;
His trousers short, through many a season true,
Made no pretence to hide his stockings blue;
A waistcoat buff his chief adornment was,
Its porcelain buttons rimmed with dusky brass.
A deacon he, you saw it in each limb,
And well he knew to deacon-off a hymn,
Or lead the choir through all its wandering
    woes
With voice that gathered unction in his nose,
Wherein a constant snuffle you might hear,
As if with him 't were winter all the year.
At pew-head sat he with decorous pains,
In sermon-time could foot his weekly gains,
Or, with closed eyes and heaven-abstracted air,
Could plan a new investment in long-prayer.
A pious man, and thrifty too, he made
The psalms and prophets partners in his trade,
And in his orthodoxy straitened more
As it enlarged the business at his store;
He honored Moses, but, when gain he planned,
Had his own notion of the Promised Land.

    " Soon as the winter made the sledding good,
From far around the farmers hauled him wood,
For all the trade had gathered 'neath his thumb.
He paid in groceries and New England rum,

Making two profits with a conscience clear, —
Cheap all he bought, and all he paid with dear.
With his own mete-wand measuring every load,
Each somehow had diminished on the road;
An honest cord in Jethro still would fail
By a good foot upon the Deacon's scale,
And, more to abate the price, his gimlet eye
Would pierce to cat-sticks that none else could spy;
Yet none dared grumble, for no farmer yet
But New Year found him in the Deacon's debt.

" While the first snow was mealy under feet,
A team drawled creaking down Quompegan street.
Two cords of oak weighed down the grinding sled,
And cornstalk fodder rustled overhead;
The oxen's muzzles, as they shouldered through,
Were silver-fringed; the driver's own was blue
As the coarse frock that swung below his knee.
Behind his load for shelter waded he;
His mittened hands now on his chest he beat,
Now stamped the stiffened cowhides of his feet,
Hushed as a ghost's; his armpit scarce could hold
The walnut whipstock slippery-bright with cold.
What wonder if, the tavern as he past,
He looked and longed, and stayed his beasts at last,
Who patient stood and veiled themselves in steam
While he explored the bar-room's ruddy gleam?

" Before the fire, in want of thought profound,
There sat a brother-townsman weather-bound:
A sturdy churl, crisp-headed, bristly-eared,
Red as a pepper; 'twixt coarse brows and beard

His eyes lay ambushed, on the watch for fools,
Clear, gray, and glittering like two bay-edged pools;
A shifty creature, with a turn for fun,
Could swap a poor horse for a better one, —
He 'd a high-stepper always in his stall;
Liked far and near, and dreaded therewithal.
To him the in-comer, ' Perez, how d' ye do ? '
' Jest as I 'm mind to, Obed ; how do you ? '
Then, his eyes twinkling such swift gleams as run
Along the levelled barrel of a gun
Brought to his shoulder by a man you know
Will bring his game down, he continued, ' So,
I s'pose you 're haulin' wood ?   But you 're too late ;
The Deacon 's off; Old Splitfoot could n't wait ;
He made a bee-line las' night in the storm
To where he won't need wood to keep him warm.
'Fore this he 's treasurer of a fund to train
Young imps as missionaries ; hopes to gain
That way a contract that he has in view
For fireproof pitchforks of a pattern new.
It must have tickled him, all drawbacks weighed,
To think he stuck the Old One in a trade;
His soul, to start with, was n't worth a carrot,
And all he 'd left 'ould hardly serve to swear at.'

" By this time Obed had his wits thawed out,
And, looking at the other half in doubt,
Took off his fox-skin cap to scratch his head,
Donned it again, and drawled forth, ' Mean he 's
          dead ? '
' Jesso ; he 's dead and t'other *d* that follers
With folks that never love a thing but dollars.

He pulled up stakes last evening, fair and square,
And ever since there 's been a row Down There.
The minute the old chap arrived, you see,
Comes the Boss-devil to him, and says he,
" What are you good at? Little enough, I fear;
We callilate to make folks useful here."
" Well," says old Bitters, " I expect I can
Scale a fair load of wood with e'er a man."
" Wood we don't deal in; but perhaps you 'll suit,
Because we buy our brimstone by the foot :
Here, take this measurin'-rod, as smooth as sin,
And keep a reckonin' of what loads comes in.
You 'll not want business, for we need a lot
To keep the Yankees that you send us hot ;
At firin' up they 're barely half as spry
As Spaniards or Italians, though they 're dry ;
At first we have to let the draught on stronger,
But, heat 'em through, they seem to hold it longer."

" 'Bitters he took the rod, and pretty soon
A teamster comes, whistling an ex-psalm tune.
A likelier chap you would n't ask to see,
No different, but his limp, from you or me —'
' No different, Perez ! Don't your memory fail ?
Why, where in thunder was his horns and tail ? '
' They 're only worn by some old-fashioned pokes ;
They mostly aim at looking just like folks.
Sech things are scarce as queues and top-boots
        here ;
'T would spoil their usefulness to look too queer.
Ef you could always know 'em when they come,
They 'd get no purchase on you : now be mum.

On come the teamster, smart as Davy Crockett,
Jinglin' the red-hot coppers in his pocket,
And clost behind ('t was gold-dust, you 'd ha'
    sworn),
A load of sulphur yallower 'n seed-corn;
To see it wasted as it is Down There
Would make a Friction-Match Co. tear its hair!
" Hold on!" says Bitters, " stop right where you be;
You can't go in athout a pass from me."
" All right," says t'other, " only step round smart;
I must be home by noon-time with the cart."
Bitters goes round it sharp-eyed as a rat,
Then with a scrap of paper on his hat
Pretends to cipher. " By the public staff,
That load scarce rises twelve foot and a half."
" There 's fourteen foot and over," says the driver,
" Worth twenty dollars, ef it 's worth a stiver;
Good fourth-proof brimstone, that 'll make 'em
    squirm, —
I leave it to the Headman of the Firm;
After we masure it, we always lay
Some on to allow for settlin' by the way.
Imp and full-grown, I 've carted sulphur here,
And gi'n fair satisfaction, thirty year."
With that they fell to quarrellin' so loud
That in five minutes they had drawed a crowd,
And afore long the Boss, who heard the row,
Comes elbowin' in with " What 's to pay here now?"
Both parties heard, the measurin'-rod he takes,
And of the load a careful survey makes.
" Sence I have bossed the business here," says he,
" No fairer load was ever seen by me."

Then, turnin' to the Deacon, " You mean cuss,
None óf your old Quompegan tricks with us !
They won't do here: we 're plain old-fashioned folks,
And don't quite understand that kind o' jokes.
I know this teamster, and his pa afore him,
And the hard-working Mrs. D. that bore him ;
He would n't soil his conscience with a lie,
Though he might get the custom-house thereby.
Here, constable, take Bitters by the queue,
And clap him into furnace ninety-two,
And try this brimstone on him ; if he's bright,
He 'll find the masure honest afore night.
He is n't worth his fuel, and I 'll bet
The parish oven has to take him yet ! " '

" This is my tale, heard twenty years ago
From Uncle Reuben, as the logs burned low,
Touching the walls and ceiling with that bloom
That makes a rose's calyx of a room.
I could not give his language, wherethrough ran
The gamy flavor of the bookless man
Who shapes a word before the fancy cools,
As lonely Crusoe improvised his tools.
I liked the tale, — 't was like so many told
By Rutebeuf and his brother ·Trouvères bold ;
Nor were the hearers much unlike to theirs,
Men unsophisticate, rude-nerved as bears.
Ezra is gone and his large-hearted kind,
The landlords of the hospitable mind ;
Good Warriner of Springfield was the last ;
An inn is now a vision of the past ;
One yet-surviving host my mind recalls, —
You 'll find him if you go to Trenton Falls."

THE ORIGIN OF DIDACTIC POETRY

WHEN wise Minerva still was young
  And just the least romantic,
Soon after from Jove's head she flung
  That preternatural antic,
'T is said, to keep from idleness
  Or flirting, those twin curses,
She spent her leisure, more or less,
  In writing po ——, no, verses.

How nice they were! to rhyme with *far*
  A kind *star* did not tarry;
The metre, too, was regular
  As schoolboy's dot and carry;
And full they were of pious plums,
  So extra-super-moral, —
For sucking Virtue's tender gums
  Most tooth-enticing coral.

A clean, fair copy she prepares,
  Makes sure of moods and tenses,
With her own hand, — for prudence spares
  A man-(or woman-)-uensis;
Complete, and tied with ribbons proud,
  She hinted soon how cosy a
Treat it would be to read them loud
  After next day's Ambrosia.

The Gods thought not it would amuse
  So much as Homer's Odyssees,
But could not very well refuse
  The properest of Goddesses;
So all sat round in attitudes
  Of various dejection,
As with a *hem!* the queen of prudes
  Began her grave prelection.

At the first pause Zeus said, " Well sung! —
  I mean — ask Phœbus, — *he* knows."
Says Phœbus, " Zounds! a wolf's among
  Admetus's merinos!
Fine! very fine! but I must go;
  They stand in need of me there;
Excuse me!" snatched his stick, and so
  Plunged down the gladdened ether.

With the next gap, Mars said, " For me
  Don't wait, — naught could be finer,
But I'm engaged at half past three, —
  A fight in Asia Minor!"
Then Venus lisped, " I'm sorely tried,
  These duty-calls are vip'rous;
But I *must* go; I have a bride
  To see about in Cyprus."

Then Bacchus, — " I must say good-bye,
  Although my peace it jeopards;
I meet a man at four, to try
  A well-broke pair of leopards."

His words woke Hermes. " Ah ! " he said,
" I *so* love moral theses ! "
Then winked at Hebe, who turned red,
    And smoothed her apron's creases.

Just then Zeus snored, — the Eagle drew
    His head the wing from under ;
Zeus snored, — o'er startled Greece there flew
    The many-volumed thunder.
Some augurs counted nine, some, ten ;
    Some said 't was war, some, famine,
And all, that other-minded men
    Would get a precious ———.

Proud Pallas sighed, " It will not do ;
    Against the Muse I 've sinned, oh ! "
And her torn rhymes sent flying through
    Olympus's back window.
Then, packing up a peplus clean,
    She took the shortest path thence,
And opened, with a mind serene,
    A Sunday-school in Athens.

The verses ? Some in ocean swilled,
    Killed every fish that bit to 'em ;
Some Galen caught, and, when distilled,
    Found morphine the residuum ;
But some that rotted on the earth
    Sprang up again in copies,
And gave two strong narcotics birth,
    Didactic verse and poppies.

Years after, when a poet asked
   The Goddess's opinion,
As one whose soul its wings had tasked
   In Art's clear-aired dominion,
" Discriminate," she said, " betimes ;
   The Muse is unforgiving ;
Put all your beauty in your rhymes,
   Your morals in your living."

THE FLYING DUTCHMAN

Don't believe in the Flying Dutchman ?
   I 've known the fellow for years ;
My button I 've wrenched from his clutch, man :
   I shudder whenever he nears !

He 's a Rip van Winkle skipper,
   A Wandering Jew of the sea,
Who sails his bedevilled old clipper
   In the wind's eye, straight as a bee.

Back topsails ! you can't escape him ;
   The man-ropes stretch with his weight,
And the queerest old toggeries drape him,
   The Lord knows how long out of date !

Like a long-disembodied idea
   (A kind of ghost plentiful now),
He stands there ; you fancy you see a
   Coeval of Teniers or Douw.

v

He greets you; would have you take letters:
   You scan the addresses with dread,
While he mutters his *donners* and *wetters*, —
   They 're all from the dead to the dead!

You seem taking time for reflection,
   But the heart fills your throat with a jam,
As you spell in each faded direction
   An ominous ending in *dam*.

Am I tagging my rhymes to a legend?
   That were changing green turtle to mock:
No, thank you! I 've found out which wedge-end
   Is meant for the head of a block.

The fellow I have in my mind's eye
   Plays the old Skipper's part here on shore,
And sticks like a burr, till he finds I
   Have got just the gauge of his bore.

This postman 'twixt one ghost and t'other,
   With last dates that smell of the mould,
I have met him (O man and brother,
   Forgive me!) in azure and gold.

In the pulpit I 've known of his preaching,
   Out of hearing behind the time,
Some statement of Balaam's impeaching,
   Giving Eve a due sense of her crime.

I have seen him some poor ancient thrashing
   Into something (God save us!) more dry,
With the Water of Life itself washing
   The life out of earth, sea, and sky.

O dread fellow mortal, get newer
    Despatches to carry, or none!
We're as quick as the Greek and the Jew were
    At knowing a loaf from a stone.

Till the couriers of God fail in duty,
    We shan't ask a mummy for news,
Nor sate the soul's hunger for beauty
    With your drawings from casts of a Muse.

CREDIDIMUS JOVEM REGNARE

    O DAYS endeared to every Muse,
    When nobody had any Views,
    Nor, while the cloudscape of his mind
    By every breeze was new designed,
    Insisted all the world should see
    Camels or whales where none there be!
    O happy days, when men received
    From sire to son what all believed,
    And left the other world in bliss,
    Too busy with bedevilling this!

    Beset by doubts of every breed
    In the last bastion of my creed,
    With shot and shell for Sabbath-chime,
    I watch the storming-party climb,
    Panting (their prey in easy reach),
    To pour triumphant through the breach

In walls that shed like snowflakes tons
Of missiles from old-fashioned guns,
But crumble 'neath the storm that pours
All day and night from bigger bores.
There, as I hopeless watch and wait
The last life-crushing coil of Fate,
Despair finds solace in the praise
Of those serene dawn-rosy days
Ere microscopes had made us heirs
To large estates of doubts and snares,
By proving that the title-deeds,
Once all-sufficient for men's needs,
Are palimpsests that scarce disguise
The tracings of still earlier lies,
Themselves as surely written o'er
An older fib erased before.

So from these days I fly to those
That in the landlocked Past repose,
Where no rude wind of doctrine shakes
From bloom-flushed boughs untimely flakes
Where morning's eyes see nothing strange,
No crude perplexity of change,
And morrows trip along their ways
Secure as happy yesterdays.
Then there were rulers who could trace
Through heroes up to gods their race,
Pledged to fair fame and noble use
By veins from Odin filled or Zeus,
And under bonds to keep divine
The praise of a celestial line.
Then priests could pile the altar's sods,

With whom gods spake as they with gods,
And everywhere from haunted earth
Broke springs of wonder, that had birth
In depths divine beyond the ken
And fatal scrutiny of men;
Then hills and groves and streams and seas
Thrilled with immortal presences,
Not too ethereal for the scope
Of human passion's dream or hope.

Now Pan at last is surely dead,
And King No-Credit reigns instead,
Whose officers, morosely strict,
Poor Fancy's tenantry evict,
Chase the last Genius from the door,
And nothing dances any more.
Nothing? Ah, yes, our tables do,
Drumming the Old One's own tattoo,
And, if the oracles are dumb,
Have we not mediums? Why be glum?

Fly thither? Why, the very air
Is full of hindrance and despair!
Fly thither? But I cannot fly;
My doubts enmesh me if I try,
Each Liliputian, but, combined,
Potent a giant's limbs to bind.
This world and that are growing dark;
A huge interrogation mark,
The Devil's crook episcopal,
Still borne before him since the Fall,
Blackens with its ill-omened sign

The old blue heaven of faith benign.
Whence ? Whither ? Wherefore ? How ?
       Which ? Why ?
All ask at once, all wait reply.
Men feel old systems cracking under 'em ;
Life saddens to a mere conundrum
Which once Religion solved, but she
Has lost — has Science found ? — the key.

What was snow-bearded Odin, trow,
The mighty hunter long ago,
Whose horn and hounds the peasant hears
Still when the Northlights shake their spears?
Science hath answers twain, I 've heard ;
Choose which you will, nor hope a third ;
Whichever box the truth be stowed in,
There 's not a sliver left of Odin.
Either he was a pinchbrowed thing,
With scarcely wit a stone to fling,
A creature both in size and shape
Nearer than we are to the ape,
Who hung sublime with brat and spouse
By tail prehensile from the boughs,
And, happier than his maimed descendants,
The culture-curtailed *in*dependents,
Could pluck his cherries with both paws,
And stuff with both his big-boned jaws ;
Or else the core his name enveloped
Was from a solar myth developed,
Which, hunted to its primal shoot,
Takes refuge in a Sanskrit root,
Thereby to instant death explaining

The little poetry remaining.
Try it with Zeus, 't is just the same;
The thing evades, we hug a name;
Nay, scarcely that, — perhaps a vapor
Born of some atmospheric caper.
All Lemprière's fables blur together
In cloudy symbols of the weather,
And Aphrodite rose from frothy seas
But to illustrate such hypotheses.
With years enough behind his back,
Lincoln will take the selfsame track,
And prove, hulled fairly to the cob,
A mere vagary of Old Prob.
Give the right man a solar myth,
And he 'll confute the sun therewith.

They make things admirably plain,
But one hard question *will* remain :
If one hypothesis you lose,
Another in its place you choose,
But, your faith gone, O man and brother,
Whose shop shall furnish you another ?
One that will wash, I mean, and wear,
And wrap us warmly from despair ?
While they are clearing up our puzzles,
And clapping prophylactic muzzles
On the Actæon's hounds that sniff
Our devious track through But and If,
Would they 'd explain away the Devil
And other facts that won't keep level,
But rise beneath our feet or fail,
A reeling ship's deck in a gale !

God vanished long ago, iwis,
A mere subjective synthesis;
A doll, stuffed out with hopes and fears,
Too homely for us pretty dears,
Who want one that conviction carries,
Last make of London or of Paris.
He gone, I felt a moment's spasm,
But calmed myself with Protoplasm,
A finer name, and, what is more,
As enigmatic as before;
Greek, too, and sure to fill with ease
Minds caught in the Symplegades
Of soul and sense, life's two conditions,
Each baffled with its own omniscience.
The men who labor to revise
Our Bibles will, I hope, be wise,
And print it without foolish qualms
Instead of God in David's psalms:
Noll had been more effective far
Could he have shouted at Dunbar,
" Rise, Protoplasm ! " No dourest Scot
Had waited for another shot.

And yet I frankly must confess
A secret unforgivingness,
And shudder at the saving chrism
Whose best New Birth is Pessimism;
My soul — I mean the bit of phosphorus
That fills the place of what that was for us —
Can't bid its inward bores defiance
With the new nursery-tales of science.
What profits me, though doubt by doubt,

As nail by nail, be driven out,
When every new one, like the last,
Still holds my coffin-lid as fast?
Would I find thought a moment's truce,
Give me the young world's Mother Goose
With life and joy in every limb,
The chimney-corner tales of Grimm!

Our dear and admirable Huxley
Cannot explain to me why ducks lay,
Or, rather, how into their eggs
Blunder potential wings and legs
With will to move them and decide
Whether in air or lymph to glide.
Who gets a hair's-breadth on by showing
That Something Else set all a-going?
Farther and farther back we push
From Moses and his burning bush;
Cry, " Art Thou there? " Above, below,
All Nature mutters *yes* and *no!*
'T is the old answer : we're agreed
Being from Being must proceed,
Life be Life's source. I might as well
Obey the meeting-house's bell,
And listen while Old Hundred pours
Forth through the summer-opened doors,
From old and young. I hear it yet,
Swelled by bass-viol and clarinet,
While the gray minister, with face
Radiant, let loose his noble bass.
If Heaven it reached not, yet its roll
Waked all the echoes of the soul,

And in it many a life found wings
To soar away from sordid things.
Church gone and singers too, the song
Sings to me voiceless all night long,
Till my soul beckons me afar,
Glowing and trembling like a star.
Will any scientific touch
With my worn strings achieve as much?

I don't object, not I, to know
My sires were monkeys, if 't was so;
I touch my ear's collusive tip
And own the poor-relationship.
That apes of various shapes and sizes
Contained their germs that all the prizes
Of senate, pulpit, camp, and bar win
May give us hopes that sweeten Darwin.
Who knows but from our loins may spring
(Long hence) some winged sweet-throated thing
As much superior to us
As we to Cynocephalus?

This is consoling, but, alas,
It wipes no dimness from the glass
Where I am flattening my poor nose,
In hope to see beyond my toes.
Though I accept my pedigree,
Yet where, pray tell me, is the key
That should unlock a private door
To the Great Mystery, such no more?
Each offers his, but one nor all
Are much persuasive with the wall
That rises now, as long ago,

Between I wonder and I know,
Nor will vouchsafe a pin-hole peep
At the veiled Isis in its keep.
Where is no door, I but produce
My key to find it of no use.
Yet better keep it, after all,
Since Nature's economical,
And who can tell but some fine day
(If it occur to her) she may,
In her good will to you and me,
Make door and lock to match the key?

TEMPORA MUTANTUR

THE world turns mild; democracy, they say,
Rounds the sharp knobs of character away,
And no great harm, unless at grave expense
Of what needs edge of proof, the moral sense;
For man or race is on the downward path
Whose fibre grows too soft for honest wrath,
And there's a subtle influence that springs
From words to modify our sense of things.
A plain distinction grows obscure of late:
Man, if he will, may pardon; but the State
Forgets its function if not fixed as Fate.
So thought our sires: a hundred years ago,
If men were knaves, why, people called them so,
And crime could see the prison-portal bend
Its brow severe at no long vista's end.
In those days for plain things plain words would serve;
Men had not learned to admire the graceful swerve

Wherewith the Æsthetic Nature's genial mood
Makes public duty slope to private good ;
No muddled conscience raised the saving doubt ;
A soldier proved unworthy was drummed out,
An officer cashiered, a civil servant
(No matter though his piety were fervent)
Disgracefully dismissed, and through the land
Each bore for life a stigma from the brand
Whose far-heard hiss made others more averse
To take the facile step from bad to worse.
The Ten Commandments had a meaning then,
Felt in their bones by least considerate men,
Because behind them Public Conscience stood,
And without wincing made their mandates good.
But now that " Statesmanship" is just a way
To dodge the primal curse and make it pay,
Since office means a kind of patent drill
To force an entrance to the Nation's till,
And peculation something rather less
Risky than if you spelt it with an *s* ;
Now that to steal by law is grown an art,
Whom rogues the sires, their milder sons call smart,
And " slightly irregular " dilutes the shame
Of what had once a somewhat blunter name,
With generous curve we draw the moral line :
Our swindlers are permitted to resign ;
Their guilt is wrapped in deferential names,
And twenty sympathize for one that blames.
Add national disgrace to private crime,
Confront mankind with brazen front sublime,
Steal but enough, the world is unsevere, —
Tweed is a statesman, Fisk a financier ;

Invent a mine, and be — the Lord knows what;
Secure, at any rate, with what you 've got.
The public servant who has stolen or lied,
If called on, may resign with honest pride :
As unjust favor put him in, why doubt
Disfavor as unjust has turned him out?
Even if indicted, what is that but fudge
To him who counted-in the elective judge?
Whitewashed, he quits the politician's strife
At ease in mind, with pockets filled for life :
His " lady " glares with gems whose vulgar blaze
The poor man through his heightened taxes pays,
Himself content if one huge Kohinoor
Bulge from a shirt-front ampler than before,
But not too candid, lest it haply tend
To rouse suspicion of the People's Friend.
A public meeting, treated at his cost,
Resolves him back more virtue than he lost ;
With character regilt he counts his gains;
What 's gone was air, the solid good remains ;
For what is good, except what friend and foe
Seem quite unanimous in thinking so,
The stocks and bonds which, in our age of loans,
Replace the stupid pagan's stocks and stones?
With choker white, wherein no cynic eye
Dares see idealized a hempen tie,
At parish-meetings he conducts in prayer,
And pays for missions to be sent elsewhere ;
On 'Change respected, to his friends endeared,
Add but a Sunday-school class, he 's revered,
And his too early tomb will not be dumb
To point a moral for our youth to come.

   1872.

IN THE HALFWAY HOUSE

I

AT twenty we fancied the blest Middle Ages
   A spirited cross of romantic and grand,
All templars and minstrels and ladies and pages,
   And love and adventure in Outre-Mer land ;
But ah, where the youth dreamed of building a minster,
   The man takes a pew and sits reckoning his pelf,
And the Graces wear fronts, the Muse thins to a
      spinster,
    When Middle-Age stares from one's glass at one-
      self !

II

Do you twit me with days when I had an Ideal,
   And saw the sear future through spectacles green ?
Then find me some charm, while I look round and
     see all
    These fat friends of forty, shall keep me nineteen ;
Should we go on pining for chaplets of laurel
    Who 've paid a perruquier for mending our thatch,
Or, our feet swathed in baize, with our Fate pick a
      quarrel,
    If, instead of cheap bay-leaves, she sent a dear
      scratch ?

III

We called it our Eden, that small patent-baker,
  When life was half moonshine and half Mary
        Jane;
But the butcher, the baker, the candlestick-maker! —
  Did Adam have duns and slip down a back-lane?
Nay, after the Fall did the modiste keep coming
  With last styles of fig-leaf to Madam Eve's bower?
Did Jubal, or whoever taught the girls thrumming,
  Make the patriarchs deaf at a dollar the hour?

IV

As I think what I was, I sigh *Desunt nonnulla!*
  Years are creditors Sheridan's self could not bilk;
But then, as my boy says, "What right has a fullah
  To ask for the cream, when himself spilt the
        milk?"
Perhaps when you're older, my lad, you'll discover
  The secret with which Auld Lang Syne there is
        gilt, —
Superstition of old man, maid, poet, and lover, —
  That cream rises thickest on milk that was spilt!

V

We sailed for the moon, but, in sad disillusion,
  Snug under Point Comfort are glad to make fast,
And strive (sans our glasses) to make a confusion
  'Twixt our rind of green cheese and the moon of
        the past.

Ah, Might-have-been, Could-have-been, Would-have-
    been ! rascals,
  He 's a genius or fool whom ye cheat at two-
    score,
And the man whose boy-promise was likened to Pas-
    cal's
  Is thankful at forty they don't call him bore !

VI

With what fumes of fame was each confident pate
    full !
  How rates of insurance should rise on the Charles !
And which of us now would not feel wisely grate-
    ful,
  If his rhymes sold as fast as the Emblems of
    Quarles ?
E'en if won, what 's the good of Life's medals and
    prizes ?
  The rapture 's in what never was or is gone ;
That we missed them makes Helens of plain Ann
    Elizys,
  For the goose of To-day still is Memory's swan.

VII

And yet who would change the old dream for new
    treasure ?
  Make not youth's sourest grapes the best wine of
    our life ?
Need he reckon his date by the Almanac's measure
  Who is twenty lifelong in the eyes of his wife ?

Ah, Fate, should I live to be nonagenarian,
    Let me still take Hope's frail I. O. U.'s upon
       trust,
Still talk of a trip to the Islands Macarian,
    And still climb the dream-tree for — ashes and
       dust !

AT THE BURNS CENTENNIAL

JANUARY 1859

I

A HUNDRED years ! they 're quickly fled,
    With all their joy and sorrow ;
Their dead leaves shed upon the dead,
    Their fresh ones sprung by morrow !
And still the patient seasons bring
    Their change of sun and shadow ;
New birds still sing with every spring,
    New violets spot the meadow.

II

A hundred years ! and Nature's powers
    No greater grown nor lessened !
They saw no flowers more sweet than ours,
    No fairer new moon's crescent.
Would she but treat us poets so,
    So from our winter free us,
And set our slow old sap aflow
    To sprout in fresh ideas !

V

III

Alas, think I, what worth or parts
  Have brought me here competing,
To speak what starts in myriad hearts
  With Burns's memory beating!
Himself had loved a theme like this;
  Must I be its entomber?
No pen save his but 's sure to miss
  Its pathos or its humor.

IV

As I sat musing what to say,
  And how my verse to number,
Some elf in play passed by that way,
  And sank my lids in slumber;
And on my sleep a vision stole,
  Which I will put in metre,
Of Burns's soul at the wicket-hole
  Where sits the good Saint Peter.

V

The saint, methought, had left his post
  That day to Holy Willie,
Who swore, " Each ghost that comes shall toast
  In brunstane, will he, nill he;
There 's nane need hope with phrases fine
  Their score to wipe a sin frae;
I 'll chalk a sign, to save their tryin', —
  A hand ( ) and ' *Vide infra!* ' "

VI

Alas! no soil's too cold or dry
    For spiritual small potatoes,
Scrimped natures, spry the trade to ply
    Of *diaboli advocatus*;
Who lay bent pins in the penance-stool
    Where Mercy plumps a cushion,
Who've just one rule for knave and fool,
    It saves so much confusion!

VII

So when Burns knocked, Will knit his brows,
    His window gap made scanter,
And said, " Go rouse the other house;
    We lodge no Tam O'Shanter!"
" *We* lodge!" laughed Burns. "Now well I see
    Death cannot kill old nature;
No human flea but thinks that he
    May speak for his Creator!

VIII

" But, Willie, friend, don't turn me forth,
    Auld Clootie needs no gauger;
And if on earth I had small worth,
    You've let in worse, I'se wager!"
" Na, nane has knockit at the yett
    But found me hard as whunstane;
There's chances yet your bread to get
    Wi Auld Nick, gaugin' brunstane."

IX

Meanwhile, the Unco' Guid had ta'en
   Their place to watch the process,
Flattening in vain on many a pane
   Their disembodied noses.
Remember, please, 't is all a dream;
   One can't control the fancies
Through sleep that stream with wayward gleam,
   Like midnight's boreal dances.

X

Old Willie's tone grew sharp 's a knife:
   " *In primis*, I indite ye,
For makin' strife wi' the water o' life,
   And preferrin' *aqua vitae!* "
Then roared a voice with lusty din,
   Like a skipper's when 't is blowy,
" If *that* 's a sin, *I* 'd ne'er got in,
   As sure as my name 's Noah! "

XI

Baulked, Willie turned another leaf, —
   " There 's many here have heard ye,
To the pain and grief o' true belief,
   Say hard things o' the clergy! "
Then rang a clear tone over all, —
   " One plea for him allow me:
I once heard call from o'er me, ' Saul,
   Why persecutest thou me? ' "

XII

To the next charge vexed Willie turned,
　　And, sighing, wiped his glasses:
" I 'm much concerned to find ye yearned
　　O'er-warmly tow'rd the lasses!"
Here David sighed; poor Willie's face
　　Lost all its self-possession:
" I leave this case to God's own grace;
　　It baffles *my* discretion!"

XIII

Then sudden glory round me broke,
　　And low melodious surges
Of wings whose stroke to splendor woke
　　Creation's farthest verges;
A cross stretched, ladder-like, secure
　　From earth to heaven's own portal,
Whereby God's poor, with footing sure,
　　Climbed up to peace immortal.

XIV

I heard a voice serene and low
　　(With my heart I seemed to hear it)
Fall soft and slow as snow on snow,
　　Like grace of the heavenly spirit;
As sweet as over new-born son
　　The croon of new-made mother,
The voice begun, " Sore tempted one!"
　　Then, pausing, sighed, " Our brother!

XV

" If not a sparrow fall, unless
    The Father sees and knows it,
Think ! recks he less his form express,
    The soul his own deposit ?
If only dear to Him the strong,
    That never trip nor wander,
Where were the throng whose morning song
    Thrills His blue arches yonder ?

XVI

" Do souls alone clear-eyed, strong-kneed,
    To Him true service render,
And they who need His hand to lead,
    Find they His heart untender ?
Through all your various ranks and fates
    He opens doors to duty,
And he that waits there at your gates
    Was servant of His Beauty.

XVII

" The Earth must richer sap secrete,
    (Could ye in time but know it !)
Must juice concrete with fiercer heat,
    Ere she can make her poet ;
Long generations go and come,
    At last she bears a singer,
For ages dumb of senses numb
    The compensation-bringer !

XVIII

" Her cheaper broods in palaces
 She raises under glasses,
But souls like these, heav'n's hostages,
 Spring shelterless as grasses :
They share Earth's blessing and her bane,
 The common sun and shower;
What makes your pain to them is gain,
 Your weakness is their power.

XIX

" These larger hearts must feel the rolls
 Of stormier-waved temptation;
These star-wide souls between their poles
 Bear zones of tropic passion.
He loved much! — that is gospel good,
 Howe'er the text you handle;
From common wood the cross was hewed,
 By love turned priceless sandal.

XX

" If scant his service at the kirk,
 He *paters* heard and *aves*
From choirs that lurk in hedge and birk,
 From blackbird and from mavis;
The cowering mouse, poor unroofed thing,
 In him found Mercy's angel;
The daisy's ring brought every spring
 To him Love's fresh evangel!

XXI

" Not he the threatening texts who deals
    Is highest 'mong the preachers,
But he who feels the woes and weals
    Of all God's wandering creatures.
He doth good work whose heart can find
    The spirit 'neath the letter;
Who makes his kind of happier mind,
    Leaves wiser men and better.

XXII

" They make Religion be abhorred
    Who round with darkness gulf her;
And think no word can please the Lord
    Unless it smell of sulphur.
Dear Poet-heart, that childlike guessed
    The Father's loving kindness,
Come now to rest! Thou didst His hest,
    If haply 't was in blindness! "

XXIII

Then leapt heaven's portals wide apart,
    And at their golden thunder
With sudden start I woke, my heart
    Still throbbing-full of wonder.
" Father," I said, " 't is known to Thee
    How Thou thy saints preparest;
But this I see, — Saint Charity
    Is still the first and fairest! "

XXIV

Dear Bard and Brother! let who may
   Against thy faults be railing,
(Though far, I pray, from us be they
   That never had a failing!)
One toast I 'll give, and that not long,
   Which thou wouldst pledge if present, —
To him whose song, in nature strong,
   Makes man of prince and peasant!

IN AN ALBUM

THE misspelt scrawl, upon the wall
By some Pompeian idler traced,
In ashes packed (ironic fact!)
Lies eighteen centuries uneffaced,
While many a page of bard and sage,
Deemed once mankind's immortal gain,
Lost from Time's ark, leaves no more mark
Than a keel's furrow through the main.

O Chance and Change! our buzz's range
Is scarcely wider than a fly's;
Then let us play at fame to-day,
To-morrow be unknown and wise;
And while the fair beg locks of hair,
And autographs, and Lord knows what,
Quick! let us scratch our moment's match,
Make our brief blaze, and be forgot!

Too pressed to wait, upon her slate
Fame writes a name or two in doubt ;
Scarce written, these no longer please,
And her own finger rubs them out :
It may ensue, fair girl, that you
Years hence this yellowing leaf may see,
And put to task, your memory ask
In vain, " This Lowell, who was he ? "

AT THE COMMENCEMENT DINNER

1866

ACKNOWLEDGING A TOAST TO THE SMITH PROFESSOR

I RISE, Mr. Chairman, as both of us know,
With the impromptu I promised you three weeks
    ago,
Dragged up to my doom by your might and my
    mane,
To do what I vowed I 'd do never again ;
And I feel like your good honest dough when
    possest
By a stirring, impertinent devil of yeast.
" You must rise," says the leaven. " I can't," says
    the dough ;
" Just examine my bumps, and you 'll see it 's no go."
" But you must," the tormentor insists, " 't is all
    right ;
You must rise when I bid you, and, what 's more,
    be light."

'T is a dreadful oppression, this making men speak
What they 're sure to be sorry for all the next week;
Some poor stick requesting, like Aaron's, to bud
Into eloquence, pathos, or wit in cold blood,
As if the dull brain that you vented your spite on
Could be got, like an ox, by mere poking, to
      Brighton.

They say it is wholesome to rise with the sun,
And I dare say it may be if not overdone
(I think it was Thomson who made the remark
'T was an excellent thing in its way — for a lark);
But to rise after dinner and look down the meeting
On a distant (as Gray calls it) prospect of Eating,
With a stomach half full and a cerebrum hollow
As the tortoise-shell ere it was strung for Apollo,
Under contract to raise anerithmon gelasma
With rhymes so hard hunted they gasp with the
      asthma,
And jokes not much younger than Jethro's phylac-
      teries,
Is something I leave you yourselves to characterize.

I 've a notion, I think, of a good dinner speech,
Tripping light as a sandpiper over the beach,
Swerving this way and that as the wave of the mo-
      ment
Washes out its slight trace with a dash of whim's
      foam on 't,
And leaving on memory's rim just a sense
Something graceful had gone by, a live present
      tense;

Not poetry, — no, not quite that, but as good,
A kind of winged prose that could fly if it would.
'T is a time for gay fancies as fleeting and vain
As the whisper of foam-beads on fresh-poured cham-
       pagne,
Since dinners were not perhaps strictly designed
For manœuvring the heavy dragoons of the mind.
When I hear your set speeches that start with a
       pop,
Then wander and maunder, too feeble to stop,
With a vague apprehension from popular rumor
There used to be something by mortals called humor,
Beginning again when you thought they were done,
Respectable, sensible, weighing a ton,
And as near to the present occasions of men
As a Fast Day discourse of the year eighteen ten,
I — well, I sit still, and my sentiments smother,
For am I not also a bore and a brother?

And a toast, — what should that be? Light, airy,
       and free,
The foam-Aphrodite of Bacchus's sea,
A fancy-tinged bubble, an orbed rainbow-stain,
That floats for an instant 'twixt goblet and brain;
A breath-born perfection, half something, half
       naught,
And breaks if it strike the hard edge of a thought.
Do you ask me to make such? Ah no, not so sim-
       ple;
Ask Apelles to paint you the ravishing dimple
Whose shifting enchantment lights Venus's cheek,
And the artist will tell you his skill is to seek;

Once fix it, 't is naught, for the charm of it rises
From the sudden bopeeps of its smiling surprises.
I 've tried to define it, but what mother's son
Could ever yet do what he knows should be done?
My rocket has burst, and I watch in the air
Its fast-fading heart's-blood drop back in despair;
Yet one chance is left me, and, if I am quick,
I can palm off, before you suspect me, the stick.

Now since I 've succeeded — I pray do not frown —
To Ticknor's and Longfellow's classical gown,
And profess four strange languages, which, luckless
　　　elf,
I speak like a native (of Cambridge) myself,
Let me beg, Mr. President, leave to propose
A sentiment treading on nobody's toes,
And give, in such ale as with pump-handles *we* brew,
Their memory who saved us from all talking He-
　　　brew, —
A toast that to deluge with water is good,
For in Scripture they come in just after the flood:
I give you the men but for whom, as I guess, sir,
Modern languages ne'er could have had a professor,
The builders of Babel, to whose zeal the lungs
Of the children of men owe confusion of tongues;
And a name all-embracing I couple therewith,
Which is that of my founder — the late Mr. Smith.

A PARABLE

An ass munched thistles, while a nightingale
From passion's fountain flooded all the vale.
" Hee-haw ! " cried he, " I hearken," as who knew
For such ear-largess humble thanks were due.
" Friend," said the wingëd pain, " in vain you bray,
Who tunnels bring, not cisterns, for my lay ;
None but his peers the poet rightly hear,
Nor mete we listeners by their length of ear."
Colonna, Italy, 1852.

EPIGRAMS

SAYINGS

I

In life's small things be resolute and great
To keep thy muscle trained: know'st thou when
      Fate
Thy measure takes, or when she'll say to thee,
"I find thee worthy; do this deed for me"?

II

A camel-driver, angry with his drudge,
Beating him, called him hunchback; to the hind
Thus spake a dervish: "Friend, the Eternal Judge
Dooms not His work, but ours, the crooked mind."

III

Swiftly the politic goes: is it dark? — he borrows a
      lantern;
Slowly the statesman and sure, guiding his steps by
      the stars.

IV

"Where lies the capital, pilgrim, seat of who gov-
      erns the Faithful?"
"Thither my footsteps are bent: it is where Saadi is
      lodged."

INSCRIPTIONS

FOR A BELL AT CORNELL UNIVERSITY

I CALL as fly the irrevocable hours,
    Futile as air or strong as fate to make
Your lives of sand or granite; awful powers,
    Even as men choose, they either give or take.

FOR A MEMORIAL WINDOW TO SIR WALTER RALEIGH, SET UP IN ST. MARGARET'S, WESTMINSTER, BY AMERICAN CONTRIBUTORS

THE New World's sons, from England's breasts we
    drew
Such milk as bids remember whence we came;
Proud of her Past wherefrom our Present grew,
    This window we inscribe with Raleigh's name.

PROPOSED FOR A SOLDIERS' AND SAILORS' MONUMENT IN BOSTON

To those who died for her on land and sea,
That she might have a country great and free,
Boston builds this: build ye her monument
In lives like theirs, at duty's summons spent.

A MISCONCEPTION

B, TAUGHT by Pope to do his good by stealth,
'Twixt participle and noun no difference feeling,
In office placed to serve the Commonwealth,
Does himself all the good he can by stealing.

THE BOSS

SKILLED to pull wires, he baffles Nature's hope,
Who sure intended him to stretch a rope.

SUN–WORSHIP

IF I were the rose at your window,
Happiest rose of its crew,
Every blossom I bore would bend inward,
They 'd know where the sunshine grew.

CHANGED PERSPECTIVE

FULL oft the pathway to her door
I 've measured by the selfsame track,
Yet doubt the distance more and more,
'T is so much longer coming back !

v

WITH A PAIR OF GLOVES LOST IN A WAGER

WE wagered, she for sunshine, I for rain,
And I should hint sharp practice if I dared;
For was not she beforehand sure to gain
Who made the sunshine we together shared?

SIXTY–EIGHTH BIRTHDAY

As life runs on, the road grows strange
With faces new, and near the end
The milestones into headstones change,
'Neath every one a friend.

INTERNATIONAL COPYRIGHT

IN vain we call old notions fudge,
    And bend our conscience to our dealing;
The Ten Commandments will not budge,
    And stealing will continue stealing.

LAST POEMS

The following note was prefixed to this group when published in 1895: " This little volume contains those of the poems which Mr. Lowell wrote in his last years which, I believe, he might have wished to preserve. Three of them were published before his death. Of the rest, two appear here for the first time. C. E. N.''

HOW I CONSULTED THE ORACLE OF
THE GOLDFISHES

WHAT know we of the world immense
Beyond the narrow ring of sense?
What should we know, who lounge about
The house we dwell in, nor find out,
Masked by a wall, the secret cell
Where the soul's priests in hiding dwell?
The winding stair that steals aloof
To chapel-mysteries 'neath the roof?

It lies about us, yet as far
From sense sequestered as a star
New launched its wake of fire to trace
In secrecies of unprobed space,
Whose beacon's lightning-pinioned spears
Might earthward haste a thousand years
Nor reach it. So remote seems this
World undiscovered, yet it is
A neighbor near and dumb as death,
So near, we seem to feel the breath
Of its hushed habitants as they
Pass us unchallenged, night and day.

Never could mortal ear nor eye
By sound or sign suspect them nigh,
Yet why may not some subtler sense
Than those poor two give evidence?

Transfuse the ferment of their being
Into our own, past hearing, seeing,
As men, if once attempered so,
Far off each other's thought can know?
As horses with an instant thrill
Measure their rider's strength of will?
Comes not to all some glimpse that brings
Strange sense of sense-escaping things?
Wraiths some transfigured nerve divines?
Approaches, premonitions, signs,
Voices of Ariel that die out
In the dim No Man's Land of Doubt?

Are these Night's dusky birds? Are these
Phantasmas of the silences
Outer or inner? — rude heirlooms
From grovellers in the cavern-glooms,
Who in unhuman Nature saw
Misshapen foes with tusk and claw,
And with those night-fears brute and blind
Peopled the chaos of their mind,
Which, in ungovernable hours,
Still make their bestial lair in ours?

Were they, or were they not? Yes; no;
Uncalled they come, unbid they go,
And leave us fumbling in a doubt
Whether within us or without
The spell of this illusion be
That witches us to hear and see
As in a twi-life what it will,
And hath such wonder-working skill

That what we deemed most solid-wrought
Turns a mere figment of our thought,
Which when we grasp at in despair
Our fingers find vain semblance there,
For Psyche seeks a corner-stone
Firmer than aught to matter known.

Is it illusion? Dream-stuff? Show
Made of the wish to have it so?
'T were something even, though this were all:
So the poor prisoner, on his wall
Long gazing, from the chance designs
Of crack, mould, weather-stain, refines
New and new pictures without cease,
Landscape, or saint, or altar-piece:
But these are Fancy's common brood
Hatched in the nest of solitude;
This is Dame Wish's hourly trade,
By our rude sires a goddess made.
Could longing, though its heart broke, give
Trances in which we chiefly live?
Moments that darken all beside,
Tearfully radiant as a bride?
Beckonings of bright escape, of wings
Purchased with loss of baser things?
Blithe truancies from all control
Of Hylë, outings of the soul?

The worm, by trustful instinct led,
Draws from its womb a slender thread,
And drops, confiding that the breeze
Will waft it to unpastured trees:

So the brain spins itself, and so
Swings boldly off in hope to blow
Across some tree of knowledge, fair
With fruitage new, none else shall share:
Sated with wavering in the Void,
It backward climbs, so best employed,
And, where no proof is nor can be,
Seeks refuge with Analogy;
Truth's soft half-sister, she may tell
Where lurks, seld-sought, the other's well.
With metaphysic midges sore,
My Thought seeks comfort at her door,
And, at her feet a suppliant cast,
Evokes a spectre of the past.
Not such as shook the knees of Saul,
But winsome, golden-gay withal, —
Two fishes in a globe of glass,
That pass, and waver, and re-pass,
And lighten that way, and then this,
Silent as meditation is.
With a half-humorous smile I see
In this their aimless industry,
These errands nowhere and returns
Grave as a pair of funeral urns,
This ever-seek and never-find,
A mocking image of my mind.
But not for this I bade you climb
Up from the darkening deeps of time:
Help me to tame these wild day-mares
That sudden on me unawares.
Fish, do your duty, as did they
Of the Black Island far away

In life's safe places, — far as you
From all that now I see or do.
You come, embodied flames, as when
I knew you first, nor yet knew men ;
Your gold renews my golden days,
Your splendor all my loss repays.

'T is more than sixty years ago
Since first I watched your to-and-fro ;
Two generations come and gone
From silence to oblivion,
With all their noisy strife and stress
Lulled in the grave's forgivingness,
While you unquenchably survive
Immortal, almost more alive.
I watched you then a curious boy,
Who in your beauty found full joy,
And, by no problem-debts distrest,
Sate at life's board, a welcome guest.
You were my sister's pets, not mine ;
But Property's dividing line
No hint of dispossession drew
On any map my simplesse knew ;
O golden age, not yet dethroned !
What made me happy, that I owned ;
You were my wonders, you my Lars,
In darkling days my sun and stars,
And over you entranced I hung,
Too young to know that I was young.
Gazing with still unsated bliss,
My fancies took some shape like this :
" I have my world, and so have you,
A tiny universe for two,

A bubble by the artist blown,
Scarcely more fragile than our own,
Where you have all a whale could wish,
Happy as Eden's primal fish.
Manna is dropt you thrice a day
From some kind heaven not far away,
And still you snatch its softening crumbs,
Nor, more than we, think whence it comes.
No toil seems yours but to explore
Your cloistered realm from shore to shore;
Sometimes you trace its limits round,
Sometimes its limpid depths you sound,
Or hover motionless midway,
Like gold-red clouds at set of day;
Ere long you whirl with sudden whim
Off to your globe's most distant rim,
Where, greatened by the watery lens,
Methinks no dragon of the fens
Flashed huger scales against the sky,
Roused by Sir Bevis or Sir Guy,
And the one eye that meets my view,
Lidless and strangely largening, too,
Like that of conscience in the dark,
Seems to make me its single mark.
What a benignant lot is yours
That have an own All-out-of-doors,
No words to spell, no sums to do,
No Nepos and no parlyvoo!
How happy you without a thought
Of such cross things as Must and Ought, —
I too the happiest of boys
To see and share your golden joys!"

So thought the child, in simpler words,
Of you his finny flocks and herds;
Now, an old man, I bid you rise
To the fine sight behind the eyes,
And, lo, you float and flash again
In the dark cistern of my brain.
But o'er your visioned flames I brood
With other mien, in other mood;
You are no longer there to please,
But to stir argument, and tease
My thought with all the ghostly shapes
From which no moody man escapes.
Diminished creature, I no more
Find Fairy-land beside my door,
But for each moment's pleasure pay
With the *quart d'heure* of Rabelais!

I watch you in your crystal sphere,
And wonder if you see and hear
Those shapes and sounds that stir the wide
Conjecture of the world outside;
In your pent lives, as we in ours,
Have you surmises dim of powers,
Of presences obscurely shown,
Of lives a riddle to your own,
Just on the senses' outer verge,
Where sense-nerves into soul-nerves merge,
Where we conspire our own deceit
Confederate in deft Fancy's feat,
And the fooled brain befools the eyes
With pageants woven of its own lies?
But *are* they lies? Why more than those

Phantoms that startle your repose,
Half seen, half heard, then flit away,
And leave you your prose-bounded day?

The things ye see as shadows I
Know to be substance ; tell me why
My visions, like those haunting you,
May not be as substantial too.
Alas, who ever answer heard
From fish, and dream-fish too ? Absurd !
Your consciousness I half divine,
But you are wholly deaf to mine.
Go, I dismiss you ; ye have done
All that ye could ; our silk is spun :
Dive back into the deep of dreams,
Where what is real is what seems !
Yet I shall fancy till my grave
Your lives to mine a lesson gave ;
If lesson none, an image, then,
Impeaching self-conceit in men
Who put their confidence alone
In what they call the Seen and Known.
How seen ? How known ? As through your glass
Our wavering apparitions pass
Perplexingly, then subtly wrought
To some quite other thing by thought.
Here shall my resolution be :
The shadow of the mystery
Is haply wholesomer for eyes
That cheat us to be overwise,
And I am happy in my right
To love God's darkness as His light.

TURNER'S OLD TÉMÉRAIRE

UNDER A FIGURE SYMBOLIZING THE CHURCH

THOU wast the fairest of all man-made things;
The breath of heaven bore up thy cloudy wings,
And, patient in their triple rank,
The thunders crouched about thy flank,
Their black lips silent with the doom of kings.

The storm-wind loved to rock him in thy pines,
And swell thy vans with breath of great designs;
Long-wildered pilgrims of the main
By thee relaid their course again,
Whose prow was guided by celestial signs.

How didst thou trample on tumultuous seas,
Or, like some basking sea-beast stretched at
       ease,
Let the bull-fronted surges glide
Caressingly along thy side,
Like glad hounds leaping by the huntsman's knees!

Heroic feet, with fire of genius shod,
In battle's ecstasy thy deck have trod,
While from their touch a fulgor ran
Through plank and spar, from man to man,
Welding thee to a thunderbolt of God.

Now a black demon, belching fire and steam,
Drags thee away, a pale, dismantled dream,
And all thy desecrated bulk
Must landlocked lie, a helpless hulk,
To gather weeds in the regardless stream.

Woe 's me, from Ocean's sky-horizoned air
To this! Better, the flame-cross still aflare,
Shot-shattered to have met thy doom
Where thy last lightnings cheered the gloom,
Than here be safe in dangerless despair.

Thy drooping symbol to the flagstaff clings,
Thy rudder soothes the tide to lazy rings,
Thy thunders now but birthdays greet,
Thy planks forget the martyrs' feet,
Thy masts what challenges the sea-wind brings.

Thou a mere hospital, where human wrecks,
Like winter-flies, crawl those renownèd decks,
Ne'er trodden save by captive foes,
And wonted sternly to impose
God's will and thine on bowed imperial necks!

Shall nevermore, engendered of thy fame,
A new sea-eagle heir thy conqueror name,
And with commissioned talons wrench
From thy supplanter's grimy clench
His sheath of steel, his wings of smoke and
        flame?

This shall the pleased eyes of our children see ;
For this the stars of God long even as we ;
Earth listens for his wings : the Fates
Expectant lean ; Faith cross-propt waits,
And the tired waves of Thought's insurgent sea.

ST. MICHAEL THE WEIGHER

STOOD the tall Archangel weighing
All man's dreaming, doing, saying,
All the failure and the pain,
All the triumph and the gain,
In the unimagined years,
Full of hopes, more full of tears,
Since old Adam's hopeless eyes
Backward searched for Paradise,
And, instead, the flame-blade saw
Of inexorable Law.

Waking, I beheld him there,
With his fire-gold, flickering hair,
In his blinding armor stand,
And the scales were in his hand :
Mighty were they, and full well
They could poise both heaven and hell.
" Angel," asked I humbly then,
" Weighest thou the souls of men ?
That thine office is, I know."
" Nay," he answered me, " not so ;

But I weigh the hope of Man
Since the power of choice began,
In the world, of good or ill."
Then I waited and was still.

In one scale I saw him place
All the glories of our race,
Cups that lit Belshazzar's feast,
Gems, the lightning of the East,
Kublai's sceptre, Cæsar's sword,
Many a poet's golden word,
Many a skill of science, vain
To make men as gods again.

In the other scale he threw
Things regardless, outcast, few,
Martyr-ash, arena sand,
Of St. Francis' cord a strand,
Beechen cups of men whose need
Fasted that the poor might feed,
Disillusions and despairs
Of young saints with grief-grayed hairs,
Broken hearts that brake for Man.

Marvel through my pulses ran
Seeing then the beam divine
Swiftly on this hand decline,
While Earth's splendor and renown.
Mounted light as thistledown.

A VALENTINE

LET others wonder what fair face
  Upon their path shall shine,
And, fancying half, half hoping, trace
  Some maiden shape of tenderest grace
    To be their Valentine.

Let other hearts with tremor sweet
  One secret wish enshrine
That Fate may lead their happy feet
  Fair Julia in the lane to meet
    To be their Valentine.

But I, far happier, am secure ;
  I know the eyes benign,
The face more beautiful and pure
  Than Fancy's fairest portraiture
    That mark my Valentine.

More than when first I singled thee,
  This only prayer is mine, —
That, in the years I yet shall see,
  As, darling, in the past, thou 'lt be
    My happy Valentine.

AN APRIL BIRTHDAY — AT SEA

On this wild waste, where never blossom came,
   Save the white wind-flower in the billow's cap,
Or those pale disks of momentary flame,
    Loose petals dropped from Dian's careless lap,
      What far-fetched influence all my fancy fills
      With singing birds and dancing daffodils?

Why, 't is her day whom jocund April brought,
   And who brings April with her in her eyes;
It is her vision lights my lonely thought,
    Even as a rose that opes its hushed surprise
      In sick men's chambers, with its glowing breath
      Plants Summer at the glacier edge of Death.

Gray sky, sea gray as mossy stones on graves; —
   Anon comes April in her jollity;
And, dancing down the bleak vales 'tween the waves,
    Makes them green glades for all her flowers and me.
      The gulls turn thrushes, charmed are sea and sky
      By magic of my thought, I know not why.

Ah, but I know, for never April's shine,
   Nor passion gust of rain, nor all her flowers
Scattered in haste, were seen so sudden fine
    As she in various mood, on whom the powers
      Of happiest stars in fair conjunction smiled
      To bless the birth of April's darling child.

LOVE AND THOUGHT

WHAT hath Love with Thought to do?
Still at variance are the two.
Love is sudden, Love is rash,
Love is like the levin flash,
Comes as swift, as swiftly goes,
And his mark as surely knows.

Thought is lumpish, Thought is slow,
Weighing long 'tween yes and no;
When dear Love is dead and gone,
Thought comes creeping in anon,
And, in his deserted nest,
Sits to hold the crowner's quest.

Since we love, what need to think?
Happiness stands on a brink
Whence too easy 't is to fall
Whither 's no return at all;
Have a care, half-hearted lover,
Thought would only push her over!

THE NOBLER LOVER

If he be a nobler lover, take him!
  You in you I seek, and not myself;
Love with men's what women choose to make
      him,
  Seraph strong to soar, or fawn-eyed elf:
All I am or can, your beauty gave it,
  Lifting me a moment nigh to you,
And my bit of heaven, I fain would save it —
  Mine I thought it was, I never knew.

What you take of me is yours to serve you,
  All I give, you gave to me before;
Let him win you! If I but deserve you,
  I keep all you grant to him and more:
You shall make me dare what others dare not,
  You shall keep my nature pure as snow,
And a light from you that others share not
  Shall transfigure me where'er I go.

Let me be your thrall! However lowly
  Be the bondsman's service I can do,
Loyalty shall make it high and holy;
  Naught can be unworthy, done for you.
Men shall say, " A lover of this fashion
  Such an icy mistress well beseems."
Women say, " Could we deserve such passion,
  We might be the marvel that he dreams."

ON HEARING A SONATA OF BEET-
HOVEN'S PLAYED IN THE NEXT
ROOM

UNSEEN Musician, thou art sure to please,
For those same notes in happier days I heard
Poured by dear hands that long have never stirred
Yet now again for me delight the keys :
Ah me, to strong illusions such as these
What are Life's solid things ?   The walls that
      gird
Our senses, lo, a casual scent or word
Levels, and 't is the soul that hears and sees !
Play on, dear girl, and many be the years
Ere some grayhaired survivor sit like me
And, for thy largess pay a meed of tears
Unto another who, beyond the sea
Of Time and Change, perhaps not sadly
      hears
A music in this verse undreamed by thee !

VERSES

INTENDED TO GO WITH A POSSET-DISH TO MY DEAR
LITTLE GOD-DAUGHTER 1882

It is of interest to know that the god-daughter was a child
of the late Sir Leslie Stephen.

In good old times, which means, you know,
The time men wasted long ago,
And we must blame our brains or mood
If that we squander seems less good,
In those blest days when wish was act
And fancy dreamed itself to fact,
Godfathers used to fill with guineas
The cups they gave their pickaninnies,
Performing functions at the chrism
Not mentioned in the Catechism.
No millioner, poor I fill up
With wishes my more modest cup,
Though had I Amalthea's horn
It should be hers, the newly born.
Nay, shudder not! I should bestow it
So brimming full she could n't blow it.
Wishes are n't horses: true, but still
There are worse roadsters than good will.
And so I wish my darling health,
And just to round my couplet, wealth,
With faith enough to bridge the chasm
'Twixt Genesis and Protoplasm,

And bear her o'er life's current vext
From this world to a better next,
Where the full glow of God puts out
Poor Reason's farthing candle, Doubt.
I 've wished her healthy, wealthy, wise,
What more can godfather devise?
But since there 's room for countless wishes
In these old-fashioned posset-dishes,
I 'll wish her from my plenteous store
Of those commodities two more,
Her father's wit, veined through and through
With tenderness that Watts (but whew!
Celia 's aflame, I mean no stricture
On his Sir Josh-surpassing picture) —
I wish her next, and 't is the soul
Of all I 've dropt into the bowl,
Her mother's beauty — nay, but two
So fair at once would never do.
Then let her but the half possess,
Troy was besieged ten years for less.
Now if there 's any truth in Darwin,
And we from what was, all we are win,
I simply wish the child to be
A sample of Heredity,
Enjoying to the full extent
Life's best, the Unearned Increment
Which Fate her Godfather to flout
Gave *him* in legacies of gout.
Thus, then, the cup is duly filled;
Walk steady, dear, lest all be spilled.

ON A BUST OF GENERAL GRANT

This poem is the last, so far as is known, written by Mr.
Lowell. He laid it aside for revision, leaving two of the verses
incomplete. In a pencilled fragment of the poem the first
verse appears as follows :

"Strong, simple, silent, such are Nature's Laws."

In the final copy, from which the poem is now printed, the
verse originally stood :

"Strong, steadfast, silent are the   laws."

but "steadfast" is crossed out, and "simple" written above.

A similar change is made in the ninth verse of the stanza,
where "simpleness" is substituted for "steadfastness." The
change from "steadfast" to "simple" was not made, prob-
ably through oversight, in the first verse of the second stanza.
There is nothing to indicate what epithet Mr. Lowell would
have chosen to complete the first verse of the third stanza.

C. E. N.

STRONG, simple, silent are the [steadfast] laws
That sway this universe, of none withstood,
Unconscious of man's outcries or applause,
Or what man deems his evil or his good;
And when the Fates ally them with a cause
That wallows in the sea-trough and seems lost,
Drifting in danger of the reefs and sands
Of shallow counsels, this way, that way, tost,
Strength, silence, simpleness, of these three strands
They twist the cable shall the world hold fast
To where its anchors clutch the bed-rock of the
        Past.

Strong, simple, silent, therefore such was he
Who helped us in our need ; the eternal law
That who can saddle Opportunity
Is God's elect, though many a mortal flaw
May minish him in eyes that closely see,
Was verified in him : what need we say
Of one who made success where others failed,
Who, with no light save that of common day,
Struck hard, and still struck on till Fortune quailed,
But that (so sift the Norns) a desperate van
Ne'er fell at last to one who was not wholly man.

A face all prose where Time's [benignant] haze
Softens no raw edge yet, nor makes all fair
With the beguiling light of vanished days ;
This is relentless granite, bleak and bare,
Rough-hewn, and scornful of æsthetic phrase ;
Nothing is here for fancy, naught for dreams,
The Present's hard uncompromising light
Accents all vulgar outlines, flaws, and seams,
Yet vindicates some pristine natural right
O'ertopping that hereditary grace
Which marks the gain or loss of some time-fondled
    race.

So Marius looked, methinks, and Cromwell so,
Not in the purple born, to those they led
Nearer for that and costlier to the foe,
New moulders of old forms, by nature bred
The exhaustless life of manhood's seeds to show,
Let but the ploughshare of portentous times
Strike deep enough to reach them where they lie :

Despair and danger are their fostering climes,
And their best sun bursts from a stormy sky:
He was our man of men, nor would abate
The utmost due manhood could claim of fate.

Nothing ideal, a plain-people's man
At the first glance, a more deliberate ken
Finds type primeval, theirs in whose veins ran
Such blood as quelled the dragon in his den,
Made harmless fields, and better worlds began:
He came grim-silent, saw and did the deed
That was to do; in his master-grip
Our sword flashed joy; no skill of words could breed
Such sure conviction as that close-clamped lip;
He slew our dragon, nor, so seemed it, knew
He had done more than any simplest man might do.

Yet did this man, war-tempered, stern as steel
Where steel opposed, prove soft in civil sway;
The hand hilt-hardened had lost tact to feel
The world's base coin, and glozing knaves made
        prey
Of him and of the intrusted Commonweal;
So Truth insists and will not be denied.
We turn our eyes away, and so will Fame,
As if in his last battle he had died
Victor for us and spotless of all blame,
Doer of hopeless tasks which praters shirk,
One of those still plain men that do the world's
        rough work.

GENERAL INDEX OF FIRST LINES

GENERAL INDEX OF FIRST LINES

GENERAL INDEX OF TITLES

GENERAL INDEX OF TITLES

END OF LOWELL'S POETICAL WORKS

The Riverside Press

Electrotyped and printed by H. O. Houghton & Co.
Cambridge, Mass., U. S. A.